UNIVERSITY OF NORTH CAROLINA
STUDIES IN THE ROMANCE LANGUAGES AND LITERATURES

Number 43

THE NOVELS AND TRAVELS
OF CAMILO JOSÉ CELA

Published with aid from
the Charles Phelps Taft Memorial Fund
University of Cincinnati

THE NOVELS AND TRAVELS
of
CAMILO JOSÉ CELA

BY

ROBERT KIRSNER

CHAPEL HILL
THE UNIVERSITY OF NORTH CAROLINA PRESS

depósito legal: v. 3.041 — 1963

ARTES GRÁFICAS SOLER, S. A. — VALENCIA, 1963

ACKNOWLEDGMENTS

For their constant encouragement and counsel, I wish to express my gratitude to Professors M. J. Hubert, Professor Emeritus of Romance Languages and Literatures at the University of Cincinnati, and R. S. Willis, Emory Ford Professor of Spanish at Princeton University.

Many were the colleagues on whom I called for advice, but these two gentlemen were subjected to the entirety of the manuscript, from the first word to the last.

To don Américo Castro,
Teacher and Friend

CONTENTS

Introduction		13
I.	Spain in the Novels of Cela	16
II.	*La Familia de Pascual Duarte*	21
III.	*Pabellón de Reposo*	35
IV.	*Nuevas Andanzas y Desventuras de Lazarillo de Tormes*	47
V.	*La Colmena*	57
VI.	*Mrs. Caldwell Habla con su Hijo*	85
VII.	*La Catira*	93
VIII.	Cela's Wanderlust	100
IX.	*Viaje a la Alcarria*	102
X.	*El Gallego y su cuadrilla*	115
XI.	*Del Miño al Bidasoa*	129
XII.	*Judíos, Moros y Cristianos*	151
XIII.	*Primer Viaje Andaluz*	169
Conclusion		182
Bibliography of Cela's works		186

INTRODUCTION

The novels and books of travels of Camilo José Cela cover a period of nearly twenty years. Cela begins writing prose as an angry young man shortly after the end of the Spanish Civil War. In 1936, upon the sudden onslaught of violent carnage, as a soldier in Franco's army, he composed agonizing verses that expressed feeling for all life around him. From the first moment of his literary career, Cela has endeavored to capture the meaning of human existence with artistic objectivity. At no time has he surrendered to propaganda. The pen of Cela recognizes no allegiance other than to the totality of Spain. His wrath and his love are directed toward the Spanish people, who constitute the *materia prima* of his writings. Cela's artistic integrity has been his personal tragedy. To this date, some of his books have been denied an audience in Spain.

The genius of Cela glows amidst human destruction. His destiny cast him into a moment of history when Spain chose to embark on a path of self-immolation. As a young man of twenty during the outbreak of the war, Cela inherited the sins of his ancestors. He was to become an actor in a struggle that was prepared by other generations. His patrimony as that of all Spaniards demanded political afiliation on one side or the other. That he transcended his role as a partisan is a testimony to his sympathetic vision of man—and his experience of life as an artist.

In the turbulent course of Spanish history, the Civil War (1936-1939) represents one of the most devastating experiences of hatred and cruelty. The number of impassioned books written on the subject give testimony to the controversial nature of the divisive conflict. The passage of time has not completely assuaged the intensity of feeling. A quarter of a century of meditation and retrospection cannot justify the fratricidal savagery that was perpetrated by a people in the name of political ideologies. Even the professed objective scholarly studies on the Spanish Civil War express shock at the horror that reigned during- and after-the blood feud. Neither side can escape condemnation. There is guilt for all. The drama of Spain is the tragedy of a people.

The aftermath of the destructive struggle, a period of time which coincides with World War II, became a receptacle of wrath and vengeance. Oppressed by hunger and political persecution, the Spaniard suffered the indignities of man's inhumanity against man. Mere survival became a virtue. No longer could existence adhere to a pattern of traditional values. The War had dispelled illusions. The past had held out the promise of a «glorious» future, but in the hell of starvation there was little place for the morrow. The government's hope for an Axis victory failed to comfort—and satiate—the prostrate populace that cried out for bread. It was an era of despair, lacking in order or direction. The past was cast into oblivion; the past had not fulfilled dreams. Yet, even in this virtual Lethean state, human existence continued in defiance of physical vicissitudes. The love for life prevailed.

The literature of Cela captures the agony of a people who are destined to live among the ruins of their own devastation. Their lives must find expression in the confinements of physical and moral deterioration. The brutal reality of hunger tends to crush their spirit. Only a sense of dignity —often vague and distorted— sustains them. Life may be reduced to absurdity but never to nothingness. However senseless, however grotesque, dreams and illusions ennoble their lives.

Since Cela the man is so much a part of his literature, a few salient facts about his life may add to the understanding of his works, especially the books of travels.

Although Cela fancies himself a patriarchal *gallego*,[1] actually he is more of a *madrileño*. Since the age of nine his life has revolved around the capital. Even today, while his home is in Palma de Mallorca, he maintains another residence in Madrid. Try as he will, he has not been able to abandon completely the scene of his triumphs and disappointments. In his life as in his literature, indefinite dreams and illusions sustain him.

---

[1] A charming, if somewhat ironical, account of his childhood is found in *La Cucaña*. Camilo José Cela. *La Cucaña*. Ediciones Destino, Barcelona, 1959.

Cela was born in Galicia on May 11, 1916. His father, a customs official, was an amateur writer, who instilled in his son a love for art. Cela's mother, Camila Enmanuela Trulock Bertorini, belonged to a Galician family that absorbed English and Italian heritages. [2] Until her marriage, Cela's mother was considered English. As a child, Cela understood English; today the language of his mother seems to frighten him. [3]

Cela's schooling, it would seem, followed the usual pattern of the middle-class Spaniard. He enrolled at the University of Madrid several years before the outbreak of the Civil War. He did not have the opportunity to graduate. In November of 1937 he enlisted in the Rebel Army that sought the overthrow of the Republic. He was discharged in 1939 with the rank of corporal at the end of the war.

Cela married María del Rosario Conde Picavea on March 12, 1944. They have one child, a son, Camilo José hijo, who was born on January 17, 1946. Since 1954 they have been making their home in Palma de Mallorca. There Cela founded a journal which combines art and literary criticism, *Papeles de Son Armadans*. This publication, which Cela personally directs, contains articles, poems and short stories. In fact, it does not in any way limit the form of its content.

Cela was elected to the Spanish Royal Academy in 1957. This is an honor he esteems greatly. For one thing, it affords him a pretext for returning occasionally to his spiritual home, Madrid. Barcelona is another city he likes to visit. There he meets with publishers and editors of some of his works. Cela has lectured and travelled in England, France and Italy. His travels have enhanced his passionate hobby of collecting empty wine bottles. Each bottle represents the memory of two friends—Cela and someone else—who have shared a mutual moment of bibulous joy.

---

[2] Cela takes pride in his racial impurity. See *La Cucaña*.
[3] At any rate, that is the impression I got when I tried to show him my manuscript.

I. SPAIN IN THE NOVELS OF CELA

The vision of Spain expressed in the novels of Camilo José Cela constitutes a key to the interpretation of characters and situations. Cela's relationship to Spain is not merely that of an author toward his *patria;* it is not only a socio-political reaction on the part of the author; Cela lives Spain in its totality, as Galdós and Baroja before him, and he dramatizes his own personal feelings toward his country in terms of novelistic creation. Throughout his novels the consciousness of Spain is a motivating force in his creative process. [1]

Although the thoughts of Cela, the man, are quite naturally interwoven into the pattern of creation of Cela, the artist, this study will devote itself primarily to the consideration of the role of Spain in the novels of Cela, i.e., Spain as a literary theme. The treatment is not intended as a sociological analysis of the author's *ideas* of his country, but rather as a literary exegesis of the role that the artist's vision of Spain plays in his development of novelistic creations.

In terms of characters and situations the novels of Cela reflect the author's artistic vision of Spain. This is not a matter of cause and effect, nor juxtaposition, but rather of compenetration. Not-

---

[1] Cela's statement «escribir en España es llorar», which recalls the lament of Larra, might well suggest that Spain itself is also the object and that *escribir en España es llorar a España*. As he affirms further, «la vida del escritor, en España, es un mantenido y cotidiano llanto, un llanto que empieza pero que no termina, un llanto eterno, un infinito llanto». Camilo José Cela, *Mis Páginas Preferidas*, («La Galera de la Literatura»), Editorial Gredos, Madrid, 1956, p. 393. Spain, then, is not mere locus, a receptacle for life; it is an integral and dynamic force in the artistic life that is created in the novels of Camilo José Cela. The «endless weeping» of the author finds expression in the literary creation of Spanish life.

withstanding the literary uniqueness of the novelistic persons, they are all permeated with Hispanic values and they are definitely related to their particular environment. Be it in a negative or positive form, or perhaps submerged in a feeling of ambivalence, the characters in their inner reality take a position towards the locale that surrounds them. Whether they conquer or are conquered by their earth, the earth that is Spain flows into them and they become an integral part of Spain. That is to say, the author is not merely viewing his characters' attitude toward Spain; he is permitting them to live out their lives according to their own possibilities and aspirations. Thus, the characters embrace within their own make-up the author's vision of Spain.

The vision of Spain evolves as the development of characters unfolds. Their lives are as beautiful or as ugly as their habitat. Their possibilities are as vast or as narrow as their terrain. Their lives are as fertile or as sterile as their earth. The development of characters is integrated with the description of their environment. Yet, the persons in Cela's novels are not mere symbols. Even when viewed as abstract representations, they do not stand apart, detached from their locale. Whatever allegorical significance they may have is related to the world they inhabit. Nor are Cela's literary figures conceived as products or results of historical and geographical situations. To be sure, they are in harmony with their circumstances, but they and their circumstances are irreducible. Cela's characters live in the image of their creator's vision of Spain, but they live as artistic entities, experiencing and becoming integrated with the world around them. Their ultimate reality rests on their own novelistic experience of their circumstances.

Inasmuch as the role of Spain as a literary object is inexorably related to the creation of personages, a study of the novelistic technique is deemed essential in determining the author's vision of his *patria* and the part that this vision plays in the creative process of the novelist. There is reason to believe, as we shall see in due course, that Cela's image of Spain profoundly affects the lives he creates in his novels. More than mere «influence», it becomes the inciting force which propels his imagery and which in itself constitutes the symphonic theme of his works.

Although no author, or no other person for that matter, is completely free and emancipated from his heritage, Cela represents an explosive literary nascence, which virtually breaks with tradition. The art of Cela recognizes «stepfathers» rather than «fathers». However much it may resemble literary antecedents, it is essentially unique in its inner structure.

Cela is not, of course, the first Spanish author who confronts himself with Spain as a literary theme. Nor is there reason to believe that he will be the last. Nonetheless, any comparison that might be made between the works of Cela with those of his immediate thematic predecessors, Baroja, Galdós, and Larra would serve primarily to add to our archaeological knowledge of Spanish literary history. However interesting such a comparison might prove to be, its value would rest on superficial or external similarities and contrasts. The inner living pattern of each author is intrinsically singular. Especially in the case of Cela are we faced with an irreducible structure which largely negates patrimonial endowments.

Quite naturally, one might find in the novels of Cela qualities which may be reminiscent of the acrimony of Larra, the irony of Galdós, and the despair of Baroja. Unquestionably, there are similar notes. Cela, too, borrows from the same scale of human feeling. Yet the composition of his creations reveals a totally distinct blend. Neither the fabric nor the effect of Cela's novels follows the pattern of other writers. The art of Cela is consciously unlike that of his predecessors, who retain a sense of traditional artistic symmetry even in their opposition to existing values. In fact, their critical attitude binds them to their past. Cela, on the contrary, is intent on destroying the past. His sense of reality arises out of the attempted obliteration of history. Man gains life as he destroys. And thus, Pascual Duarte, his first novelistic protagonist, comes into being. There is no longer the concept of accepted images. Life is neither a circle nor a square, but rather the elimination of symbols. From destruction, creation.

For Mariano José de Larra (1809-1837), whose vision of Spain is intimately expressed in his *Artículos de Costumbres*, the theme of destruction is an end in itself. The obliteration of characters and existing values is his ultimate creation; and his art, with all its agonizing brutal force, remains in a state of nihilism. Novelistic characters do not emerge because their potential lives are effaced before they can be fully formed. His creative process is translated in terms of the annihilation of humanity. Not even the self is spared in this suicidal adoration.

Benito Pérez Galdós (1843-1920), who is the most direct literary heir Cervantes has had in Spain, succeeds in creating novels as he learns to blend laughter with tears. For Galdós, negativism is a youthful phase which he eventually transcends. His art matures as he dedicates himself to *living* Spain in his novels rather than to viewing it as rational matter. As life in Spain ceases to be an object for criticism and becomes a sympathetic literary theme, his uniquely Spanish characters attain a reality worthy of Cervantian creations.

Pío Baroja (1874-1956), who evoked belated debts of gratitude from writers of note in the last years of his life,[2] is the master of unfinished novelistic creations. His characters have all the possibilities of being real, but they do not achieve the end of living. They are cut off, as it were. They do not fill out their structures. What emerges as real in the novels of Baroja is the despair of his figures. The motif of hopelessness, the idealization of inaction, best represent Baroja's vision of Spain.

Cela uses destruction as a means of creation. For him, chaos is the beginning of life. But out of darkness does not come light, but more mystery. And out of chaos, confusion. Reality consists of experiencing life as a disparate agony, a suffering which has no more rhyme or reason than just being.

It would be sheer conjecture, and perhaps an oversimplification of historical circumstances, to attribute Cela's position toward Spain —and life— to the advent and aftermath of the Spanish Civil War (1936-1939). Yet, like any other intense experience of life and death, this War in which Cela was an active participant must have affected him deeply, so deeply in fact that there is a conscious effort on his part to cast it into oblivion. What is left unsaid is often more stylistically significant than that which is explicitly stated. There are

---

[2] As Baroja lay on his deathbed, Hemingway is quoted as saying to the Basque master, «Allow me to pay this small tribute to you who taught so much to those of us who wanted to be writers when we were young. I deplore the fact that you have not yet received a Nobel Prize, especially when it was given to so many who deserved it less, like me, who am only an adventurer». *Time*, October 29, 1956. Cela's eulogy to Baroja has been published in book form: *Recuerdo de Don Pío Baroja*, Ediciones de Andrea, México, 1958.

hardly any references to the Civil War in Cela's compositions.[3] Yet, his writings deal primarily with the conflict of man against man, and more precisely with man against himself. The struggle is the thing. And the more insoluble the conflict, the more beautiful the struggle. Beauty here would be synonymous with *disparity* for Cela thrives on incongruity. The characters he creates are as discordant as the world around him. The discordance, however, does not become orderly. It is discrepant, inconsistent. If there is any harmony in his themes and characters, it is precisely the variation of dissonance, the fluidity of asymmetry. There is a pattern of harrowing, impossible situations but not a sameness in the topic or the setting. Thus, the aggregate works of Cela are in themselves heterogeneous, unrelated in subject matter.[4] This distinct external dissimilarity, as well as their inner thematic unity, binds them and characterizes them as belonging to the same grotesque sphere.

In his treatment of Spain as a literary theme as in his forging of characters, Cela's artistic imagery appears to be distorted. One perceives a deliberate intent on the part of the novelist to present a vision of life which is in conflict with tradition. Thus, Spain as well as the novelistic characters, is fashioned in this form of self-contradiction. Indeed, the characters and Spain are seen in a perspective of *Gestalt*. Man and his habitat, man and his circumstances, are irreducible in the novels of Camilo José Cela. Together, in their literary image, they constitute Cela's vision of Spain, his inner experience of Spanish life.

---

[3] The references are subtly coincidental, it would seem. It is significant, for example, that Pascual Duarte, awaiting death, should make his last will and testament «en trance de muerte a 11 de mayo de 1937» although the date need not have coincided so precisely with the Civil War period. Camilo José Cela, *La Familia de Pascual Duarte*, Quinta edición, Ediciones Destino, S. L., Barcelona, 1951, p. 58.

[4] Although Cela attributes variation of themes to his desire to answer critics, it seems that for a confirmed recalcitrant person who has little feeling for literary conventions, and less for critics, the inducement was hardly adequate. See Prologue, «Algunas Palabras al que Leyere», to *Mrs. Caldwell Habla con su Hijo*, Ediciones Destino, Barcelona, 1953, pp. 9-15.

II. LA FAMILIA DE PASCUAL DUARTE

The first novel of Camilo José Cela, *La familia de Pascual Duarte* (1942), marks an explosive breach with tradition. It forms a line of demarcation with the Spanish novel of the past.[1] More than the beginning of a new movement,[2] this novel signifies a new form of art. Far more reaching in its impact than the frivolous *nivola* of Unamuno,[3] *La Familia de Pascual Duarte* shocks and stuns the reader with its seemingly senseless brutality.[4] Here we have barbarity which spares no one, not even the giver of life. Moreover, monstrosity

---

[1] Cela is intent on not writing an orthodox novel. In *La Familia de Pascual Duarte* action is commensurate with inner personal life, not with a generic concept of time. «Usted sabrá disculpar el poco orden que llevo en el relato, que por eso de seguir por la persona y no por el tiempo me hace andar saltando del principio al fin y del fin a los principios como langosta vareada, pero resulta que de manera alguna, que ésta no sea, podría llevarlo, ya que lo suelto como me sale y a las mientes me viene, sin pararme a construirlo como una novela...», p. 89. Quinta edición. Destino, Barcelona, 1951.

[2] «Los novelistas de receta, al ver que había tenido cierto buen éxito, el cierto buen éxito que pueda tener un libro en un país donde la gente es poco aficionada a leer, empezaron a seguir sus huellas y nació el tremendismo, que, entre otras cosas, es una estupidez de tomo y lomo, una estupidez sólo comparable a la estupidez del nombre que se le da.» *Mrs. Caldwell Habla con su Hijo*, p. 10.

[3] Unamuno's novel or «nivola» is clever and it is carefully contrived so as to impress the reader with its uniqueness, but the reader is aware that the author is *playing* with him in the same manner that he plays with his characters. Thus, the «nivola» is provocative but not quite serious.

[4] Pío Baroja admittedly was too frightened to write a prologue for the novel. According to Cela, this is what transpired: «Yo a Baroja le había pedido un prólogo, pero no quiso hacerlo. Después me alegré porque vi que era más elegante aparecer en cueros en primera edición. Baroja se salió como pudo. —No; mire —me dijo—, si usted quiere que lo lleven a la cárcel vaya solo, que para eso es joven. Yo no le prologo el libro. A la cárcel no fui, pero la novela fué retirada.» *La Familia de Pascual Duarte*, pp. 16-17.

does not detract from reality; on the contrary, we are repelled because we can and do project ourselves in this abhorrent situation. Our inner concealed feelings—not to say suppresed or subconscious—are reached, and we react with hostility.⁵ When the reader regains his composure, he is likely to want to dismiss the book as «just too hideous», but it is too late; the impression of disproportionate horror has already been made. The author has succeeded in transmitting to us his positive vision of an incongruous Spanish life which is experienced in terms of violence and destructiveness.⁶

Even though one can rationally attest to the senselessness of the action, the situation, and the style, the protestation will not remove the imprint of verisimilitude.⁷ To be sure, whatever disparity the plot may have, whatever inconsistencies there may be between the protagonist, the supposed narrator of the story, and the language he employs, they only serve to accentuate the reality of incongruity. *La Familia de Pascual Duarte* is deliberately disproportionate, intentionally cruel.⁸ In effect, it is logical in its structure.

In this novel Spain is presented as a sanguinary image. Blood is the unifying motif of the work. In life as in death, in love as in hate, the characters come alive through the appearance of the word *la sangre*. More than any other word or phrase, *blood* gives life to the literary figures and their circumstances. At the very beginning of the account, the characterization of Pascual suggests an ordinary picaresque-type «hero» until he bursts forth with his passion for blood.

---

[5] The publication of the book was forbidden in Spain after the second edition, which probably constituted the first careful reading that the censors undertook. «Esta edición salió en noviembre de 1943, y fue la que recogió la censura.» *Ibid.*, p. 16.

[6] Perhaps the most offensive act of the novel is to make the criminal a better person than his victims. In the words of Marañón: «Lo que da aspecto de truculencia a este relato, y esto sí es puro truco, si bien legítimo y bien logrado, es el artificio con que el autor nos distrae para que no reparemos en que Duarte es mejor persona que sus víctimas y que sus arrebatos criminosos representan una suerte de abstracta y bárbara pero innegable justicia.» *Ibid.*, Prólogo, p. 38.

[7] «La tremenda historia de Pascual Duarte, como la de los héroes griegos o la de algunos protagonistas de la gran novela rusa, es tan radicalmente humana que no pierde un solo instante el ritmo y la armonía de la verdad.» *Ibid.*, p. 37.

[8] In Cela's own words: «Cuando un ambiente está oliendo a algo, lo que hay que hacer, para que se fijen en uno, no es tratar de oler a lo mismo sólo que más fuerte, sino, simplemente, tratar de cambiar el olor.» *Ibid.*, p. 31.

Es extraño, pero de mozo, si me privaban de aquel olor [a bestia muerta] me entraban unas angustias como de muerte; me acuerdo de aquel viaje que hice a la capital por mor de las quintas; anduve todo el día de Dios desazonado, venteando los aires como un perro de caza. Cuando me fui a acostar, en la posada, olí mi pantalón de pana. *La sangre* me calentaba todo el cuerpo... Quité a un lado la almohada y apoyé la cabeza para dormir sobre mi pantalón, doblado. Dormí como una piedra aquella noche. [9]

Immediately we become aware of his literary birth. In the first few pages he was rather generic in nature. Now he is introduced as a unique person. The first chapter ends on a note of more blood, caused by what seems to be an unprovoked killing. But it is thus, through destruction in this saturnalian carnage, that Pascual Duarte is born as a novelistic character.

Un temblor recorrió todo mi cuerpo; parecía como una corriente que forzaba por salirme por los brazos. El pitillo se me había apagado; la escopeta, de un solo caño, se dejaba acariciar, lentamente, entre mis piernas. La perra seguía mirándome, fija, como si no me hubiera visto nunca, como si fuese a culparme de algo de un momento a otro, y su mirada me calentaba la sangre de las venas de tal manera que se veía llegar el momento en que tuviese que entregarme; hacía calor, un calor espantoso, y mis ojos se entornaban dominados por el mirar, como un clavo, del animal...
Cogí la escopeta y disparé; volví a cargar y volví a disparar. La perra tenía una sangre oscura y pegajosa que se extendía poco a poco por la tierra. [10]

In hatred, as when Pascual voices his resentment against don Rafael, «the friend of the family», blood again recurs as the elixir of life.

Un reló que obedecía a sus palabras, soltadas poco a poco y como con cuidado, y a sus ojillos húmedos y azules como los de las víboras, que me miraban con todo el intento de simpatizar, cuando el odio más ahogado era lo único que por

---

[9] *Ibid.*, p. 66 (the italics are mine).
[10] *Ibid.*, pp. 69, 70.

> mi sangre corría para él... Me acuerdo con disgusto de aquellas horas:
> —¡Angelitos al cielo! ¡Angelitos al cielo!... [11]

Four pages later it is a scene of intense love that is given life by the presence of the precious yet horrendous liquid of existence.

> Fue una lucha feroz. Derribada en tierra, sujeta, estaba más hermosa que nunca... Sus pechos subían y bajaban al respirar cada vez más de prisa... Yo la agarré del pelo y la tenía bien sujeta a la tierra... Ella forcejeaba, se escurría...
> La mordí hasta la sangre, hasta que estuvo rendida y dócil como una yegua joven... [12]

And again in the same episode as Pascual turns his thoughts to his dead brother, he notes the presence of blood in its exact quantity. «La tierra estaba blanda, bien me acuerdo... Y en la tierra, media docena de amapolas para mi hermano muerto: seis gotas de sangre...» [13] Blood for love, blood for life, blood for death!

Pascual's first wife, Lola, dramatically expresses the essence of his existence when she exclaims: «—Tu sangre que se vierte en la tierra al tocarla! [14] Later on, having offended him by bearing someone else's child, she offers to redeem herself by means of blood.

> Mis ojos y mi sangre, por haberte ofendido... —Es que la sangre parece como el abono de tu vida... Aquellas palabras que me quedaron grabadas en la cabeza como un fuego, y como con fuego grabadas conmigo morirán. [15]

It is now that Pascual becomes aware of the truth of his life. He must free himself from the agony of existence by the same means that he came into being. And so he seeks to avenge his dishonor by murdering «el Estirao».

> Un nido de alacranes se revolvió en mi pecho, y en cada gota de sangre de mis venas una víbora me mordía la carne...

---

[11] *Ibid.*, p. 100.
[12] *Ibid.*, p. 104.
[13] *Ibid.*, p. 104.
[14] *Ibid.*, p. 150.
[15] *Ibid.*, pp. 176-177.

> Pisé un poco más fuerte... La carne del pecho hacía el mismo ruido que si estuviera en el asador... Empezó a arrojar sangre por la boca. Cuando me levanté, se le fue la cabeza — sin fuerza — para un lado... [16]

Consequently Pascual spends three years in prison. He returns home to what appears to be a new life. He marries again, and just as serenity and social adjustment might be anticipated by the reader of traditional tales [17] (after all, the book has already abounded with cruelty and violence and only a few pages remain) Pascual experiences his last act of life before going to the gallows. Again, blood is the fascinating, exotic agent which is the breath of being, the source of life, and the expression of death.

> ... huir tampoco podía; iba indefectiblemente camino de la ruina... No había más solución que golpear, golpear sin piedad, rápidamente, para acabar lo más pronto posible...
> Entonces sí que ya no había solución. Me abalancé sobre ella y la sujeté. Forcejeó, se escurrió...
> La sangre salía como desbocada y me golpeó la cara. Estaba caliente como un vientre y sabía lo mismo que la sangre de los corderos...
> La solté y salí huyendo. Choqué con mi mujer a la salida; se le apagó el candil. Cogí el campo y corrí, corrí sin descanso, durante horas enteras. El campo estaba fresco y una sensación como de alivio me recorrió las venas... Podía respirar... [18]

Pascual Duarte has begun his narration by *not being*,[19] now life has breathed into him: «Podía respirar...»

Although externally fully formed as a man, Pascual has no life as the book begins; at the end, as he is about to lose his physical identity as a man and disappear from view, his evanescence is pregnant with reality. He can now breathe life. He has overcome its mysteries. Death frees him from all bonds of society and more significantly from himself.

---

[16] *Ibid.*, pp. 179, 185.

[17] Although it is known at the beginning of the story that Pascual is doomed to die in prison, and there is evidence that Pascual has left his home to avoid becoming an assassin, the last ten pages of this book have the suddenness of an earthquake as they follow a peaceful interlude.

[18] *Ibid.*, pp. 215-216.

[19] *Yo, señor, no soy* malo. *Ibid.*, p. 61 (the italics are mine).

In the novels of Cela little space is devoted to the description of environmental conditions *per se;* the reader acquires a vision of Spain primarily through the behavior of characters. Spain is its people. More than mere symbols—an interesting case might be made for Pascual Duarte's being an allegory of Spain—the literary persons are totally integrated with their habitat. However «universal» they may be,[20] like La Celestina, Lazarillo, or Fortunata, they are singularly Hispanic in their structure. Only in the *particular* realm of that which is Spain can we understand the actions and motivations of all characters in *La Familia de Pascual Duarte.* Even their physical situation is singularly identifiable with Spain of the post-Civil War period. Not only is the book, then, restricted to a locale but also to a period. The characters are irreducible from the time as well as the space that surrounds them. It would be an anachronism to transfer them to another era, an anatopism to place them in another land. Circumstances of time and place counterpoise the reality of the characters. Removed from their specific situations, they would be no more than caricatures, or at best, vacuous symbols.[21]

Unlike the Spain of Quevedo, Cela's Spain is not evil or inverse; unlike the defective Spain of Larra and Baroja, Cela's Spain is not viewed in judgment. Indeed, the most frighteningly impressive aspect of Cela's attitude toward his country is that it lacks moral perspective. Spain is recreated in its dynamic being. There are instances of goodness and many more of evil, but always in the course of expressive being. Good and evil are but fleeting moments of contemplation. Lives are lived, in the last analysis, in compatibility with their inner possibilities; they are not motivated by external social forces. Cela's characters are not plaintive; neither are they acquiescent. Their

---

[20] According to Marañón, «Duarte es, ... un personaje de significado universal...» *Ibid.,* p. 44, of the Prologue. His significance may be universal, but his essence is uniquely Spanish.

[21] Even when speaking of *universality,* we must remember that for characters to attain any degree of generic appreciation or universality, they must be first uniquely and individually *real.* It is through their singular form that we project ourselves and experience *einfühlung.* Othello and Don Quixote, for example, are first of all unique persons; only when that is established can we identify their *qualities* with broad, human *characteristics.* We are often reminded of their lives — parts of which we see around us, but their literary make-up, their total reality, is peculiarly and exclusively theirs. There are, undoubtedly, Quixotic and Othellian characters, but only one Don Quixote, one Othello!

seemingly asymmetrical actions, anarchichal from a collective point of view, follow an irregular pattern that is singularly their own.

The characters in *La Familia de Pascual Duarte,* even those who seem incited only by evil, are capable of experiencing moments of goodness, which are equated with beauty.

> Mario seguía tirado en el mismo sitio donde lo dejé, gimiendo por lo bajo, con la boca en la tierra y con la cicatriz más morada y miserable que cómico en cuaresma; mi hermana, que creí que iba a armar el zafarrancho, lo levantó del suelo por ponerlo recostado en la artesa... Aquel día me pareció más hermosa que nunca, con su traje de azul como el del cielo, y sus aires de madre montaraz, ella, que ni lo fuera, ni lo había de ser... [22]

There is also righteous indignation and scorn for the person who lacks feeling.

> Mi madre tampoco lloró a la muerte de su hijo; secas debiera tener las entrañas una mujer con corazón tan duro que unas lágrimas no le quedaran siquiera para señalar la desgracia de la criatura... De mí puedo decir, y no me avergüenzo de ello, que sí lloré, así como mi hermana Rosario, y que tal odio llegué a cobrar a mi madre, y tan de prisa había de crecerme, que llegué a tener miedo de mí mismo. [23]

Unlike la Celestina or Tirso's Don Juan, Pascual is not the incarnation of evil or frivolity. Just as he is about to seem proportionately wicked in our eyes, his figure undergoes permutation. If only Pascual were completely devoid of sympathy, the book would not be so horrendous!

Another significant trait that accentuates the incongrous nature of Pascual's personality and that prevents him from becoming a picaresque protagonist is that at times he displays a profound sense of honor. Not always, but occasionally, when he *feels* affronted. There are moments, then, when he appears almost as a *pundonoroso* 17th century hero.

---

[22] *Ibid.,* p. 96.
[23] *Ibid.,* pp. 97-98.

> Sí; mejor era no seguir, me lo decía la conciencia. Mejor era dejar que el tiempo pasara, que el niño naciera... Los vecinos empezarían a hablar de las andanzas de mi mujer, me mirarían de reojo, se pondrían a cuchichear en voz baja al verme pasar...
> Si mi condición de hombre me hubiera permitido perdonar, hubiera perdonado, pero el mundo es como es y el querer avanzar contra corriente no es sino un vano intento. [24]

His correlation with society does not follow a parallel line. On the matter of repentance, he clearly denies contrition.

> ... ya ni pido perdón en esta vida. ¿Para qué? Tal vez sea mejor que hagan conmigo lo que está dispuesto porque es más que probable que si no lo hicieran volviera a las andadas. No quiero pedir el indulto porque es demasiado lo malo que la vida me enseñó y mucha mi flaqueza para resistir al instinto. [25]

Instinct prevails. The pity he inspires is interwoven with horror.

Horror and pity, with very little exaltation, are also contained in the limited descriptions of environment. As time,[26] space, too, is presented personalitiscally. It is significant only as it relates to the characters' inner lives, for in *La Familia de Pascual Duarte* there is hardly any probing into external or physical reality.

> Por detrás del corral pasaba un regato, a veces medio seco y nunca demasiado lleno, cochino y maloliente como tropa de gitanos, y en el que podían cogerse unas anguilas hermosas, como yo algunas tardes y por matar el tiempo me entretenía en hacer... allá, a lo lejos, como una tortuga baja y gorda, como una culebra enroscada que temiese despegarse del suelo, Almendralejo comenzaba a encender sus luces eléctricas... Sus habitantes a buen seguro que ignoraban que yo había estado pescando, que estaba en aquel momento mismo...[27]

In effect, there is a parallel in the meagerness of outer descriptions of people and the outer descriptions of the land. In both instances,

---

[24] *Ibid.*, pp. 174-175.
[25] *Ibid.*, p. 57.
[26] See note 1.
[27] *Ibid.*, p. 67.

we are impressed by this lack. Basically, the author seems to dismiss the *milieu* as he does the particular setting of a house: «El resto de la casa no merece la pena ni describirlo, tal era su vulgaridad». But even when he does describe the abode, it is inexorably related to the people who dwell in it: «El hogar era amplio y despejado y alrededor de la campana teníamos... En las paredes teníamos...»[28] The personality of the protagonist invariably permeates the depiction of the locale.

> Era un pueblo caliente y soleado, bastante rico en olivos y guarros (con perdón), con las casas pintadas tan blancas, que aún me duele la vista al recordarlas, ... ¡qué airosa!, ¡qué elegante, no parecía a todos la fuente...! [29]

The relationship between characters and environment is not one of cause and effect as it is in naturalistic novels. The rapport here rest on compenetration. The literary persons are in sympathy with their time and space. It is a configurative presentation which is seen through the events of human existence. When the characters express anguish, for example, they are expressing an anguish that is theirs in their intimate totality, in their time and in their space.

If the lack of moral values in the lives of the characters is frightening, more disturbing still is the absence of judgment or evaluation in the recreation of contemporary Spanish society. There are no panegyrics and there are no vilifications. Provincial life in Spain here lacks the censure of the naturalist and the admiration of the romanticist. *La Familia de Pascual Duarte* neither extols nor condemns reason or emotion. In fact, nothing is reprehensible; nothing is eulogized. Life is experienced with intensity, often cruelly, but with no directive from good or evil. The feeling for life seems completely devoid of abstractions, it is profoundly personal. At times it may coincide with the reader's pre-conceived ideals; more frequently it is a dramatic departure—at least, from the *conscious*. In any case it does not seem patterned in the literary tradition of sympathy and antipathy. The book, then, is likely to produce a state of incompatibility and possibly complete rejection, on the part of the reader, who is trained to cope with good and evil but not with their virtual absence.

---

[28] *Ibid.*, pp. 64-65.
[29] *Ibid.*, p. 62.

Perhaps if the absence of moral values were complete and perfect, the book could be easily classified as amoral. What accentuates the incongruous nature of this novel is precisely the privation of consistency. It does not follow a straight line nor is it a circular one in the sense that it ends where it begins.

As we have seen, there are glimmers or at least flickers of goodness; there are expressions, however feeble, of personal and social guilt. But they do not survive. They serve to infuse the vacuum of life with foreign matter, as it were, to keep it from being a perfect vacuum. We cannot say that «nada es nada», [30] *nada es*. We are not at all sure what it may be, it may not fit any rational or emotional pattern, but it *is*.

The existentialist proclaims «L'homme est néant» [31] and thus describes a perfect vacuum, a nothingness which is absolute. In the novel of Cela not even *nothing* can complement the verb *to be*. Man is *not* nothing even if neither is he something. In effect, the verb need not link man to anything; it is self sufficient in just *being*. The essence of life is not reduced to an idea; it can only continue to be essential if it is experienced as life.

Américo Castro's profound analysis of the Hispanic *vivir desviviéndose* [32] might help us to understand the essence of life in *La Familia de Pascual Duarte*. But here it is a *vivir* without direction, certainly without ideals; it is primarily a naked *vivir*, destructive without an end. Yet, for all its negation of social ideals, life emerges as a positive force worth living. It is not reduced to a symmetrical «existentialistic» symbol. «Ya podía respirar» [33] are words which express a living experience of life—almost a hedonistic joy for human existence.

Pascual is not the only one whose life seems without purpose. Society in general appears aimless, not intent on being cruel, but yet unconcerned with kindness. It may not defend, but it certainly does

---

[30] This expression is contained in La Pardo Bazán's *El revólver*. Cuentos Españoles. Henry Holt and Co. 1950.

[31] A dramatic example of this is Sartre's *Le Diable et le Bon Dieu*.

[32] Américo Castro, *España en su Historia,* Editorial Losada, S. A., Buenos Aires, 1948, pp. 25-45. In answer to my letter in which I suggested to him that his article «Sobre España, los españoles y lo español» in *Cuadernos de Paris,* mayo-junio, 1959 «smacked» of Castro, Cela writes that he considers himself «un humilde discípulo de don Américo Castro».

[33] *Op. cit.,* p. 216.

not oppose the circumstances which surround it. If it has no paradigms of virtue, it also lacks symbols of sin. Human heights have no zenith and depths are without a nadir. In a sense, it is an attitude which is far more difficult to combat. In any case, it is more incomprehensible in rational terms, especially since there are instances of apparent human and literary conformity.

If the virtual absence of ethical values serves as a departure from tradition, the occasional inclusion of a literary technique, reminiscent of Cervantes and Galdós, adds to the irregular pattern of *La Familia de Pascual Duarte*. There are in this work, for example, instances of irony which recall the compassionate critical humor of *Don Quijote* and *Fortunata y Jacinta*. There are moments when the author's tears are filled with laughter.[34] It is interesting that Pascual, as he recounts the story of his life while awaiting execution, should display a sense of humor about the foibles of humanity. There is much acrimony in the observations of the protagonist, but there is also an element of naive wonderment that makes the reader smile.

The agents of the Church, frequently the object of ridicule and scorn in traditional censorious literature in Spain, in this novel arouse more hilarity than contempt.

Cuando acabó, me volví a la sacristía. Allí estaba don Manuel desvistiéndose.
—Tú dirás.
—Pues ya ve usted... Me quería casar.
—Me parece muy bien, hijo, me parece muy bien; para eso ha creado Dios a los hombres y a las mujeres, para la perpetuación de la especie humana.
—Sí, señor.
—Bien, bien... ¿Y con quién? ¿Con la Lola?
—Sí, señor.
—¿Y lo llevas pensando mucho tiempo?
—No, señor; ayer...
—¿Ayer nada más?
—Nada más. Ayer me dijo ella lo que había.
—¿Había algo?
—Sí...
—¿Embarazada?
—Sí, señor. Embarazada.
—Pues sí, hijo, lo mejor es que os caséis...[35]

---

[34] See note 1 of preceding chapter.
[35] *Op. Cit.,* p. 115.

> Nos habló otra vez de la perpetuación de la expecie, nos habló también del Papa León XIII, nos dijo no sé qué de San Pablo y los esclavos... ¡A fe que el hombre se traía bien preparado el discurso! [36]

The prison chaplain also appears as a sympathetic character, ingenuous and unconscious of any world outside his own. In this respect he is like the rest of the characters whose lives loom as isolated islands. For el Padre Santiago holy rites are the fulfillment of life, the joy of living. His self immersion, his absolute subjectivity, prevents him from establishing a rapport with his flock. As a result, we have before us an abyss of laughter sprinkled with tears.

> Vino un curita viejo y barbilampiño, el P. Santiago Lurueña, bondadoso y acongojado, caritativo y raído como una hormiga.
> Es el capellán el que dice la misa los domingos, esa misa que oyen un centenar de asesinos, media docena de guardias y dos pares de monjas...
> —¿Tú sabes lo que es la confesión? Me acobardada el contestar. Tuve que decir, con un hilo de voz:
> —No mucho.
> —No te preocupes hijo; nadie nace sabiendo.
> El Padre Santiago me explicó algunas cosas que no entendí del todo; sin embargo debían de ser verdad porque a verdad sonaban. [37]

The Church as an institution is neither commended nor condemned for its inherent self-protective aloofness. Its egocentricity may be ludicrous as in the aforementioned instances, but it is a position that is presented as being free of value judgment. The circumstances are neither good nor bad, they just are such as they are, mostly incongruous. At times they inspire terror, occasionally they produce laughter.

There are expressions of novelistic irony in other instances too. At times one has the fleeting impression that he is faced with Cervantian situations of simultaneous laughter and tears. Thus we laugh at deplorable conditions that we recognize as a truth of human behavior.

---

[36] *Ibid.,* p. 119.
[37] *Ibid.,* pp. 157-158.

> Ni con él ni con mi madre me atreví nunca a preguntar de cuando lo tuvieron encerrado, porque pensé que mayor prudencia sería el no meter los perros en danza, que ya por sí solos danzaban más de lo conveniente; claro es que en realidad no necesitaba preguntar nada porque como nunca faltan almas caritativas, y menos en los pueblos de tan corto personal, gentes hubo a quienes faltó tiempo para venir a contármelo todo. [38]

Illustrations of irony are found even in moments of horror. In an incident that will terminate in the gushing of human blood as though it were emanating from a spring, to quote Pascual, [39] we have these words preceding the slaughter. «Los amigos se echaron a un lado, que nunca fuera cosa de hombres meterse a evitar las puñaladas...» [40] We may smile but at the same time we are saddened by the verity of this utterance.

Similarly we are amused by Pascual's observation on civilization, as epitomized by Madrid. The protagonist is unable to comprehend the inaction of a more sophisticated society.

> Se mentaron a las madres, se llamaron a grito pelado chulos y cornudos, se ofrecieron comerse las asaduras, pero lo que es más curioso, ni se tocaron un pelo de la ropa. Yo estaba asustado viendo tan poco frecuentes costumbres... [41]

It would seem that Cela were ridiculing the Hispanic *abulia,* which the generation of 1898 took so seriously. In any case we have here another incongruity, this time between the mode of life in the capital and life in the provinces. It is not that one is superior or inferior to the other but rather that they exist in their unique ways without understanding. Blood is not easily drawn in Madrid. Pascual, who lives by it and is frightened by its absence, finds himself as an extra-social person and feels the need to return home. In his lair he may not always understand the reason for blood, but he has a feeling for it and he must live accordingly.

---

[38] *Ibid.,* pp. 71-72.
[39] «Me levanté, me fui hacia él, y antes de darle tiempo a ponerse en facha, le arreó tres navajazos que lo dejé como temblando. Cuando se lo llevaban, camino de la botica de don Raimundo, le iba manando la sangre como de un manantial...» *Ibid.,* p. 128.
[40] *Ibid.,* p. 128.
[41] *Ibid.,* p. 168.

In *La Familia de Pascual Duarte* all characters live according to their individual agonizing possibilities. In this *family*, which is in a broader sense Spain, there is an ensemble of discordant human voices which constitute an aggregation of solos rather than a chorale. The soloists are not melodious; they are not following any pre-conceived notion of harmony, not even of a contrapuntal nature. The performance is made more dissonant by unexpected displays of rhythmic sounds. If it is not completely symmetrical, neither is it entirely lacking in proportion. It cannot be encompassed by positives or negatives. The only proof of its existence is that the symphony consumes itself.

III. PABELLÓN DE REPOSO

The second novel of Cela, *Pabellón de Reposo* (1943), for all its placidness and delicacy of style, is no less horrifying than *La Familia de Pascual Duarte*. Actually, the contrast between the poetic style [1] and the morbid theme accentuates the agonizing incongruity of man's being. If the intent of the artist was to create an anti-Pascual, [2] his success is limited to external representations. The inner motif of *Pabellón de Reposo* centers on man's self-consumption. Blood, the fountain of life, contains the seeds of death. Through blood man is made aware of the nature of his devastating existence. [3]

In the first novel we have the dramatization of cruelty in action, as man is bent on destroying in order to gain life. Here we have a vision of man already in a state of virtual annihilation, as he awaits death in a sanitorium for incurable tuberculars. In both instances the emphasis is on life rather than on death. Even in the imminent arrival of death, man continues to be, to live life. Ultimate evanescence only attests to his having existed. Blood heralds his disappearance from earth, but blood also proclaims his consciousness of still being alive.

---

[1] «*Pabellón de reposo* tanto pudiera tener, puestos a hilar delgado, de novela como de poema en prosa. Su pretendidamente mantenida angustia, sin más compás de espera que un breve intermedio, así nos forzaría a considerarlo.» Camilo José Cela, *Pabellón de reposo*, Ediciones Destino, S. L., Barcelona, Octubre, 1952, (Segunda Edición). «Nota a Esta Edición.»

[2] «En *Pabellón de reposo* intenté hacer el anti-Pascual.» «Algunas Palabras al que Leyere», Introduction to *Mrs. Caldwell Habla con su Hijo*, Ediciones Destino, S. L., Barcelona, 1953, p. 10.

[3] In comparison to *La Familia de Pascual Duarte* the appearance of blood is more subdued. As a stylistic key to the interpretation of the work, it is no less significant. «...escribí *Pabellón de reposo*, que es una novela donde no pasa nada y donde no hay golpes, ni asesinatos, ni turbulentos amores, y sí tan sólo la mínima sangre...» *Ibid.*, p. 11.

Pabellón de Reposo is, in effect, the placid, poetic version of *La Familia de Pascual Duarte*. It is, in other words, the first novel elevated to the realm of calm poetry. We still have the interplay of life and death, one giving meaning to the other, but it is presented in a style that is delicately piercing. Yet, the more sensitive the mode of expression, the greater the horror. The theme and its treatment do not seem to converge; there is a lack of inherent harmony There are moments of exaltation but they are soon joined by expression of a cruel physical reality which converts the experience into a grotesque sensation.

The world of illusions, the world of absolute beauty, as it can exist in the sphere of the imagination, is joined by the realm of brutal physical reality. Tenderness and cruelty are blended.[4] The image of beauty is anamorphic. It is a fleeting sensation of exaltation; it is a feeling of pitiable terror; it is the disproportionate composition of these and other dynamic elements pleasing or unpleasing. «La vida es bella al tiempo que cruel.»[5]

Cela's imagery is not reduced to romantic simplicity. It is not a matter of contrasts. The macabre in itself is not necessarily beautiful. Thus, the flow of blood may be depressing, even repulsive. «Estoy abatido, profundamente abatido, y no ceso ni un instante de toser y de escupir sangre.»[6] Conversely, the flow of blood may be an affirmation of the joy of living.

> Volvió de nuevo el 52, pálido, demudado.
> No hay en todo el orbe hombre más hermoso. Hasta hercúleo me pareció cuando vi su torso desnudo.
> He tenido tres fuertes hemoptisis. *¡Aún tengo sangre!*[7]

The reader may wince at the character's concept of «hermoso», he may recoil at the grotesqueness of the situation, but if he is capable of enpathy, if he is sympathetically sensitive to the literary situation, he will feel the happiness of the character.

---

[4] Notwithstanding Cela's statement, «Pido perdón por disfrazar la ternura de crueldad...», rather ironical in nature, tenderness and cruelty are integral components of one another in his world. *Pabellón de Reposo*, «Nota a Esta Edición».

[5] *Ibid.*, p. 175.

[6] *Ibid.*, p. 130.

[7] *Ibid.*, p. 147. (The italics are mine).

Blood *per se,* like the life it represents, has no meaning other than just being. Its flow need not be poetic nor un-poetic It may be neither and it may be both. At times it is depicted in a quasi naturalistic manner.

> Ayer tuve un fuerte vómito de sangre.
> La señorita del 40 no me quiere. Le dio miedo verme echar sangre por la boca, casi medio cubo...
> No paro ni un instante de echar sangre. Me dicen que son extraños los casos de muerte por hemoptisis. Es posible; pero me obstino en dudarlo, en no creerlo por lo menos a ojos cerrados...
> —Ayer, ¿no sabe usted?, tuve tres esputos rojos grandes y cinco pequeños. [8]

In other instances the same prosaic words acquire poetic force. The last cited quotation, for example, becomes a musical refrain when it is repeated after the death of the character who had first uttered it. Still, in other cases there are brutal metaphors that convert the situation into poetry while retaining all aspects of forceful — and ugly — physical reality.

> Pero en su sonrisa existía una inefable belleza, que me cuesta mucho trabajo recordar. Había tenido un vómito de sangre, que vino de repente, sin avisar, y estaba pálida, bellamente pálida y con unas negras ojeras bordeando sus ojos azul claro. El pelo lo tenía revuelto sobre la almohada, y las manos caían a lo largo de su cuerpo, tan pálidas como las teclas del piano. Lloraba cuando me cogió de los hombros para decirme: ...
> Me muero por la boca, como el pez, enganchado al siniestro anzuelo que me devuelve a la tierra sangrando por la lengua... [9]

Since the references to blood have relevance to the corporeal decaying state of the subjects, they do not permit absolute exaltation. The realm of human experience is integrated with the lyrical imagery.

Cela's concept of beauty is not prohibitory. There is no *a priori* exclusion of human circumstances. Any experience of life may reach

---

[8] *Ibid.,* pp. 57, 127 and 132.
[9] *Ibid.,* pp. 52 and 159.

Elysean heights or it may descend to the nether regions of disfiguration. In both instances, which frequently occur simultaneously, equivocally, the value of the experience rests on the particular circumstantial event. Blood, ephemeral in nature, may be described in radiant terms, or it may suggest human abjection, utter abomination. In the arabesque world of Cela, the portrayal of human existence has infinite possibilities.

The depiction of cruelty, too, lacks any pre-conceived notions of eurythmy. It follows a range of feeling which is multilateral and often deliberately amphibolous. The most supreme act of cruelty in *Pabellón de Reposo* is introduced poetically in a language which is delicately musical although the situation itself is prosaic.

> En el cuarto de costura amplio, soleado, las planchadoras y las zurcidoras parlotean sin descanso.
> En un rincón, una enfermera ríe descompasadamente. Estremece oir su risa estentórea, que retumba por todo el pabellón, que quien sabe si se oirá en las habitaciones de los enfermos, de los hombres que sufren con dulzura y sin desesperanza, porque una leve lucecita de ánimo alumbra todavía en el fondo de sus corazones. [10]

Suddenly the description degenerates into a ruthless expression of human abasement.

> La enfermera tiene la bata salpicada de sangre. Ha venido a mudarse. Su aspecto es sano y robusto; el color de su tez, sonrosado; el de sus dientes, blanquecino; el de sus ojos, castaño.
> —¡Qué gracioso, Dios mío, Dios santo! Se destapó por completo para morirse; tiró la sábana al suelo y apareció en cueros vivos, bañado en sangre... ¿Sabéis lo único que tenía puesto en todo su cuerpo? No puedo casi ni hablar de risa que me da. Pues sólo los calcetines y las ligas... ¡Ja, ja, ja!
> El coro de mujeres rió con la enfermera el divertido aspecto del desgraciado que murió de una hemoptisis con las ligas puestas. A alguna costurera quizás le corriese un escalofrío de remordimiento por la espalda...
> —A ver, dadme una bata limpia, que tengo que ir a tomar las pulsaciones. [11]

---

[10] *Ibid.*, p. 115.
[11] *Ibid.*, pp. 115 and 116.

True, there is no cruelty of action in terms of murder as there is in *La Familia de Pascual Duarte*, but the cruelty of ridicule is equally, if not more, expressive of flagrant debauchery. The horror lies not on the death of the tubercular, but rather on the grotesque experience of his death by the nurse. Laughter, in this instance, is the cruelest gesture possible. If there is a more horrifying aspect yet, it is that the reader may find some humor in this episode. One sentence «A alguna costurera quizás le corriese un escalofrío de remordimiento por la espalda...» prevents this passage from deteriorating into an abyss of absolute negativism. It is the one thought that emphasizes the agony of life.

The force of cruelty is not always limited to its destructiveness. It can serve as an inspiration to poetic propensity. The following letter, received when the tubercular is already dead, reveals a certain malevolent inspiration on the part of the authoress, who resides outside of the sanitorium among the healthy in body.

> Querido amigo:
> Es inútil esa reiterada insistencia. De forma bien clara te lo he dado a entender. No tengo por qué uncirme a un carro ardiendo ni por qué embarcarme en un buque que hace agua. Si algún día te quise, olvídalo. Te saluda, A. [12]

The figures of speech may create an uninviting image, almost odious, but it is a graphic one which is indelibly imprinted on the reader. The crudeness of the language does not detract from its effect; on the contrary, it adds to its brutality.

As in *La Familia de Pascual Duarte* the greatest cruelty is inflicted by those «healthy-normal» people who do not feel life with intensity. These are the people who do not suffer the joys and sadness of life; these are the people who have no consciousness of the agony of human existence. They may not kill, but neither do they love. They are hermetical characters incapable of compenetration. They are rational and they lack the full grasp of life which can be obtained only by the consciousness of death.

> Amada mía de mi corazón: Nadie sabe como yo del amargor del cariño. Los hombres sanos, los hombres que an-

---

[12] *Ibid.*, p. 181.

> dan por la ciudad, que van y vienen a sus negocios, que se suben a los automóviles y se sientan en las cervecerías; los hombres a quienes ves a diario por las calles, nada saben de lo que es amar, de lo que significa amar apasionadamente, en una lucha titánica, feroz y desigual contra el reloj que marcha, sin piedad alguna, sin consideración de ninguna clase...
> Nada saben de lo que es amar, porque nada saben tampoco del silencioso tránsito que se alarga, casi indefinidamente, como aquellos besos que tú y yo nos dábamos sentados al pie del árbol de tu jardín, para morir un día...
> ... te quiero hasta el fin de los mundos, hasta donde se pierde la memoria, hasta donde Dios empieza y acaba, hasta el límite mismo de lo que no tiene límite. [13]

The awareness of death places the emphasis on *awareness* rather than on *death*, which is not a flamboyant romantic image.

> ¿Será la Gloria un éxtasis, una contemplación, como creemos los cristianos? ¿Será una ampliación de los tremendos placeres de la tierra, como suponen los mahometanos? ¿Será un hacerse Nada y encontrar en la negación la ansiada felicidad, como piensan los indos? [14]

Even when death seems kind, even when it may mean communion with God, it is not absolute happiness.

> ¡Ah, qué ignorantes somos y qué poco vemos más allá del alcance de nuestra primera mirada! La señorita del 37 será, quizás, dichosa en la contemplación de Dios; pero feliz, lo que se dice realmente feliz..., ¿lo será? [15]

Life is dynamic; death, static.

In spite of the intellectual atmosphere that prevails in *Pabellón de Reposo*, the novel does not deteriorate, novelistically speaking, into a philosophical symposium. Although the characters are represented by mere numbers, they are not abstractions. Their lives are uniquely tangible. It is not then rationale, but the expression of their inner experiences that give meaning to their characterization. If at times

---

[13] *Ibid.*, pp. 73 and 74.
[14] *Ibid.*, p. 145.
[15] *Ibid.*, p. 132.

they are pathetic, they are no more so than the literary persons of Cela's first novel. If they appear to be incarcerated, with death as their only means of escape, the situation is analagous to that of *La Familia de Pascual Duarte*.

The moribund patients of *Pabellón de Reposo* have in common—as do all living — the inexorable fulfillment of life. They are joined together by a realization that they are all in a state of self-consumption. The flow of blood is their bond of sympathy. Nonetheless, each tubercular lives out his life in his own distinctive manner in conformance with his peculiar possibilities. There is no magic in this secluded pavilion of repose. The ever-presence of death does not succeed in giving life a harmonious generic delineation. On the contrary, it futhers the distortion of the panorama. What the imminence of death does accomplish is to bestow upon the patients an indelible impression of the vital immensity of life that exists in any circumscribed environment, even within the walls of a sanitorium.

As in the case of their literary predecesor, destruction is the key to life. The significant difference is that whereas Pascual comes into being as he destroys, the tuberculars acquire life as they are being destroyed.

The sanitorium is a world of introspective revelation. Here, in microcosmic existence, man has a favorable climate for the expression of his being. Most patients are classified as active or passive «sufferers» but there are impenetrable exceptions in this pattern.

> Hay gentes a quienes agrada el sufrimiento. Son de dos clases: sufridoras y mortificantes. Las sufridoras gozan en la propia desgracia con un aplomo que espeluzan; las mortificantes gustan de hacer sufrir a los demás... Excepciones, ¿dónde no las hay? [16]

Some wither imperceptively, perhaps insensibly. There is an element of indefinite disproportion. Not all pieces fit. The puzzle is not solved. It continues being.

The banker undergoes a metamorphosis in his being. His sense of practicality wanes as he becomes sensitive to the truth of poetry. The virtuous girl, «la piadosa señorita que enfermó de virtudes», however, is intransmutable. She lives and dies by the *virtue* which

---

[16] *Ibid.*, pp. 118-119.

incited her sickness.[17] Yet, her characterization is as forceful and believable as that of the banker. Virtue radiates as much vitality as poetry. It is no less alive than evil, though possibly more rare in the world of Cela.

In spite of the deliberate omission of place, time, and names,[18] the setting of this novel is the world of Cela, contemporaneous with the reality of the novelist's existence, physical and imaginary. His characters live in his time and his place (Spain). If they are nameless, it is because he has found it more impressive not to have christened them. Their anonymity adds to their tangible reality. Their particular numbers, corresponding with those of their cells, are their sobriquets, their assumed appellation as they enter the realm of literary existence. The number of the room constitutes the Quixotic process of being knighted; it transforms them into characters in a book.

In this novel, as in the first one, there is little description of external reality. Cela seems intent on penetrating and expressing the inner core of Spanish human existence, casting aside irrelevant details of time and space. Only the physical experience, the description of blood, for example, that relates to the person's intimate feelings is considered worthy of attention. There is an apparent desire on the part of the writer to escape the devastating barrenness that charaterized the Spanish habitat during the first decade following the end of the Civil War. Although outwardly the sanitorium seems to exist in a mythical sphere, inwardly it is revealed as the castle of agonizing people who experience the joys and sadness of life and death in the same manner as the healthy peasants of the first novel. The atmosphere among the tuberculars is more intellectual but no less intense in its brutal expression of man's palpation of life. In both instances, as he feels his own destruction, man gropes for life and seeks identification. In both novels, his identification is only with an incongruous *being*, a *being* that defies classification. In Cela's words:

---

[17] *Ibid.*, pp. 117-118. Although her characterization is static, it recalls the ironical description of José Ido del Sagrario in *Fortunata y Jacinta* by Galdós.

[18] «Sin referencia geográfica, onomástica o temporal que permitiese su localización en una época o lugar determinados (salvo, quizá, la relativa, y siempre muy aproximada, situación en el calendario que pudiera averiguarse por las terapéuticas empleadas con mis marionetas...)» *Mrs. Cadwell habla con su hijo*, p. 11.

Vivimos en el mundo del ser, en el concreto e inexorable planeta del ser... Las cosas, queramos o no queramos, nos convenga o no nos convenga, son como son... [19]

The particular ambiance in *Pabellón de Reposo,* as in all of Cela's novels, is basically a façade. It is a disguise for the indigenous world that is Spain, that is to say, for the novelist's experience of the world that is Spain. Cela is profoundly sensitive to the multifarious masks that man assumes in his existence: «No se trata más que de la máscara, que del antifaz, que del engañador disfraz que la vida y el hombre se colocan...»[20] His literary persons, too, follow this form of deceptive dress. In their essential nakedness, however, they reveal a consanguineous existence.

Although *Pabellón de Reposo* is inexorably related to *La Familia de Pascual Duarte* in its thematic content, it possesses literary characteristics that distinguish it as a singular artistic entity. In addition to its isolation from time and place and its inventive device of relying on dehumanization (number of room) to transform the physical world into the realm of literature, *Pabellón de Reposo* is more expressive than the first novel in revealing the personality of its author. Whereas in *La Familia de Pascual Duarte* the author pretends to be a mere messenger in the creative process of Pascual's life, in the second work there is no such artifice. On the contrary, Cela twice interrupts the account to quote letters of protestation imploring him to discontinue his narrative, which first appeared in newspaper serialized form. He also includes his answers in which he proclaims his determination not to desist. In this expression of integralism in which we have a juxtaposition of literary and «flesh and blood» reality, the personality of the novelist is violently projected. His brusque entrance in the narration magnifies in form the perspective of divarication which already exists in content. The interplay of the real and the imaginary is not at all Cervantian; it lacks subtlety. It is deliberatly explosive and rude. Cela enters the scene in the fulminant manner of a Pascual Duarte and thus creates an illusion of distorted symbols.

It is now hardly possible for the composition to maintain an unbroken spell over the reader. What Cela the man, has written is

---

[19] *Mis páginas preferidas,* pp. 394-395.
[20] *Ibid.,* p. 395.

interwoven with what Cela the author, has created. The delicate descriptive thread of the tuberculars suddenly resumes, but what we are experiencing now is no longer a proportionate symbol of literature. The pattern is advisedly unsymmetrical. The presentation of an uneven world also lacks evenness.

As a writer, Cela seems more sure of himself than he did in his first novel. He already has established himself as a significant novelist who can afford the luxury of being controversial, even shocking. There is no undercurrent of apology for his style, nor for his content. The Spanish public for which he is writing may be hostile, but not unattentive. He, himself, can assume the role of the disruptive literary *agent provocateur*. Thus, in his answers to the letters that plead for the cessation of his work, Cela manifests his position as a man and as an artist. His perplexity with those who would shield cruelty and brutality is patent.

> Un conocido tisiólogo, el doctor A. M. S., viejo y admirado amigo mío, *hombre bueno si los hay* y concienzudo, estudioso y entrañable como pocos, me escribe una larga carta rogándome que suspenda la publicación de mi novela *Pabellón de Reposo*.
> La carta del doctor A. M. S. me dejó perplejo...
> Mi amigo no está en lo cierto... Mi amigo tiene una obsesión, una saludable obsesión, el restablecimiento de sus enfermos, y ve fantasmas dañinos donde sólo existen tenues e inofensivas neblinas. [21]

His literary recreation of life is not the phantom that causes its agony. He ends the letter by citing Don Quijote's words in defense of his pursuits.

> Todo es artificio y traza —decía Don Quijote— de los malignos magos que me persiguen. ¿Por qué vosotros, buenos amigos, preocupación de mi amable comunicante a quien tan poco voy a complacer, no pensáis en algo parecido? Id contra vuestros malignos y mágicos perseguidores y no entorpezcáis mi marcha. Yo os prometo que tan pronto como piense que pudiera entorpecer la vuestra, me haré a un lado del camino. [22]

---

[21] *Pabellón de Reposo*, pp. 94, 95 and 96.
[22] *Ibid.*, p. 96.

Cela's admonition to his public is pointedly mordant. The «magic» of his art rests on the reality of human experience. Eliminate cruelty, harness brutality, extirpate agony, expiate sin; in brief, cure the ills of man and his art will have no *raison d'être*. If it is his pen that is obstructing the creation of a new euphoric Spain, he will cast it aside and renounce his adventure.

The second instrusive letter, written presumably by a tubercular friend of Cela, is more personal still. We learn of Cela's participation in the Civil War and of his decoration by the Franco goverment. «...me enseñó una fotografía tuya, de militar, recién acabada *vuestra guerra,* con las insignias de tu arma en la solapa y las condecoraciones que te dió el Gobierno...» [23] The reference is ironical. Already Cela's first novel was beginning to be censored by the government that had bestowed such high honors upon him. The letter further emphasizes the chasm that exists between the novelist and the world around him. It poses a question which is applicable to all literature that is not purely mythical, if such an absolute literary state can ever exist. «¿Has reparado en el daño que puede hacernos a quienes, para nuestra desgracia, coincidimos en el doble papel de lectores y posibles protagonistas?» [24] The danger to which the work would expose a person in the dual role of reader and protagonist is the risk that any literary expression, especially a novel or drama, imposes upon its audience. The answer is implicit in the question. There is no moral consideration. The reader projects his own values in the interpretation of literature. Often, Cela affirms sardonically, he is quite wrong in his comprehension of the intent of the artist. «No lo sé a ciencia cierta; pero me imagino que no se ha dado a mis pobres personajes el sentido de que he querido rodearlos.» [25]

Cela, is, in effect, dramatizing the abyss that exists between his work and the audience to which it is directed. Actually, it is a situation which is brought about by a feeling of ambivalent *rapport*. The audience, at any rate, a good part of it, is sensitive to being the protagonist of his drama and is reacting with hostility. At the same time that there is self-pity through emotional identification, there is horror and rational rejection. The novelist knows that the denial of malice

---

[23] *Ibid.,* p. 191.
[24] *Ibid.,* p. 193.
[25] *Ibid.,* p. 194.

on this part will not assuage the grief of projection. «...si estuviera convencido —que todavía no lo estoy— de que el efecto de mis páginas fuera malévolo, hubiera puesto punto final inmediatamente.» [26] Moreover, his art is volcanic rather that palliative. Its effect is to unnerve, to shake the symmetrical foundations of his society.

The seemingly extraneous epistles that fulgurate in this work like flashes of lightning accentuate the rhythm of disproportion. If the poetic nature of the style sheltered the reader from experiencing shock, the letters return him to this disturbing state. They constitute the writer's literary «trick». They serve to reaffirm the mood of horror in this drama of self destruction. Further, and perhaps more dramatically so, they reveal the power of Cela's art in its radiation of antagonism, its creation of contrariety.

The façade of poetic abstractness in setting and style masks, but does not succeed in concealing the telluric fabric of *Pabellón de Reposo*, which is fundamentally as contemporaneously earthly as *La Familia de Pascual Duarte*. If there are any doubts, the invasive correspondence should dispel them. The frame of reference for the second novel is as much a «slice of life» as that of the first one. Indeed, if a comparison were made, *Pabellón de Reposo* would emerge as the more «realistic» of the two. Although the environment is definitely circumscript, it relates with intensity to the world of the author and the readers—Spain. The sanitorium need not be reduced to an allegorical symbol of Spain in order to allude to external conditions. In fact, its affinity with the outside world need not at all rest on outward signs of analogy. Cela is intent on expressing the inner structure of life around him. The similitude is reflected in the theme of the novel, which evokes the cacophony of Spanish life during the early forties. As with the tuberculars of the novel, the image before Cela's audience is that of self-destruction, without purpose, without meaning. The frightening aspect of Cela's works to the immediate audience is not that they reproduce faithfully, «naturalistically», the external details of environment, but rather that they reveal the innermost being of Spanish life. They constitute a mirror of truth which is unbearable and understandably rejectable. In *Pabellón de Reposo* the letters, which reflect the reaction of the public, dramatize the truth or the fear of truth that the mirror holds.

---

[26] *Ibid.*, p. 194.

IV NUEVAS ANDANZAS Y DESVENTURAS DE LAZARILLO DE TORMES

Camilo José Cela's vision of contemporary Spain irrupts in his third novel,[1] *Nuevas Andanzas y Desventuras de Lazarillo de Tormes*, in the form of historical recreation of literature—the picaresque. His position, ruthlessly presented in this genre of acrimony, is undissimulating. If *Pabellón de Reposo* is the embellishment of *La Familia de Pascual Duarte*, *Nuevas Andanzas y Desventuras de Lazarillo de Tormes* is its skeleton, its utter disfiguration. If writing is his great revenge as Cela has stated,[2] the third novel would seem to answer the accusations of excesive cruelty that characterize his first two books. The theme of human destruction through hunger, a theme which has a sense of reality in the world of Cela,[3] presents, unbelievable though it may seem, a more grotesque impression of Spain than was possible

---

[1] Although Cela purports to disregard the question of what is a novel, he is quite discriminating in the application of the term. «He coleccionado definiciones de novela, he leído todo lo que sobre esta cuestión ha caído en mis manos, he escrito algunos artículos, he pronunciado varias conferencias y he pensado constantemente y con todo el rigor de que puede ser capaz sobre el tema y, al final, me encuentro con que no sé, ni creo que sepa nadie, lo que, de verdad, es la novela. Es posible que la única definición sensata que sobre este género pudiera darse, fuera la de decir que 'novela es todo aquello que, editado en forma de libro, admite debajo del título, y entre paréntesis, la palabra *novela*'». *Mrs. Caldwell habla con su hijo*, «Algunas palabras al que leyere».

[2] *Papeles de Son Armadans*, 1957, VI (XVII).

[3] «...el tema capital de la picaresca, el hambre, que antes podía tratarse jovialmente y ser objeto de risa y algazara en una sociedad férreamente asentada sobre jerarquías de riqueza y poder inconmovibles, hoy es no menos que el tema central de la preocupación política.» Camilo José Cela, *Nuevas Andanzas y Desventuras de Lazarillo de Tormes*, Revista de Occidente, Madrid, 1948 (Segunda Edición), p. 19.

in Cela's previous works. As before, the absence of moral judgment adds a note of horror to the panorama of incongruity.

The 20th-century Lazarillo lacks the charm of his 16th-century ancestor. Even Pascual Duarte is a more sympathetic character than Cela's modern *pícaro*. Pascual Duarte has more feelings—even in his hatred—for his world than does his materialistic counterpart. Hunger, a motif that relates intimately to the reader's realm of experience, appears as a more ugly destructive force than murder. In the first two novels a poetic image of man prevailed in blood; in the spectacle of hunger, man is virtually reduced to matter. Only a consciousness of his plight prevents him from undergoing an absolute transformation in this reductive process.

La Familia de Pascual Duarte horrified its public with its mirror of introspection. The possibility that it reflected an inner truth caused revulsion and rejection. *Nuevas Andanzas y Desventuras de Lazarillo de Tormes,* an extrospective novel, is shocking in its simplicity. It beholds the realities of the physical world. The glass of its mirror is not blurred. It is crystal-clear. It reveals a Spain in turmoil, violently moved by its search for bread and unable to acquire form.

The propinquity of the theme to the realm of human experience divests the book of much poetic reality. The literary tempo is set by the magnification of the ugly and the crude. Without doubt, *Nuevas Andanzas y Desventuras de Lazarillo de Tormes* borders on the execrable. Cela seems intent on proving that there are greater cruelties than the spilling of blood, more ugliness in the world than physical harm. This is his great revenge. By means of words, in his lascivious morbidity, Lazarillo appears to be a more despicable son than Pascual in matricide. The course of this third novel rest primarily on misanthropy. Occasionally expressions of kindness, pathos, and humor disturb the march of relentless odium.

The first two works of Cela were written in blood. The horror of blood often attained heights of exaltation. It conjured poetic images. In *Nuevas Andanzas y Desventuras de Lazarillo de Tormes* the mood is venomous. It is prescribed by a cannibalistic apocalypse of Spain. The theme of destruction is crudely presented. The figuration of blood represents savage barbarity. It is dried blood. Macabre humor, an expression of conscious malice, serves to magnify the horror of hanging bodies, and hanging sausages.

En el pueblo, cuando vino el señor juez con toda su corte de curiales y su rabo de Guardia civil, se procedió diligentemente a descolgar al padre, a la madrasta y a las dos criadas del Julián; y los vecinos, no sé si para festejar Dios sabrá qué rara figuración de la sangre o si solamente por espíritu de imitación, el caso es que también empezaron a descolgar de las campanas de sus chimeneas toda suerte de morcones, jamones, lomo en tripa, chorizos, salchichas, morcillas y demás embutidos, con lo que —si a la larga perdieron los que antes habían tenido— a la corta salimos todos gananciosos y bien alimentados. [4]

No greater poison than hunger. Here the lust for physical existence is revolting. Man is reduced more thoroughly to an animal level by the hunger for subsistence than by a thirst for blood.

In presenting the nefariousness of self-preservation, *Nuevas Andanzas y Desventuras de Lazarillo de Tormes* withdraws from the plane of moral judgment, thus adding a note of panic to the horrendous view of life. The book has the format of *Lazarillo de Tormes* and much of the blatant content of *El Buscón* although it is essentially singular in its structure. It is more intensely acid than *Lazarillo de Tormes*, and less absolute in its negativism than the work of Quevedo. In reading *El Buscón* there is an awareness of denial of reality, or negation of values; in Cela's picaresque situation literary verisimilitude is not completely distorted. There exists the frightening possibility that his characters could be «true to life», that their position of ethical apathy in their quest for daily bread might reflect a truth of the reader's world.

If the novel followed a rectilinear course of virulence or if its detachment from moral judgment precluded expressions of personal human feelings, *Nuevas Andanzas y Desventuras de Lazarillo de Tormes* would emerge as an Odyssey of evil and would therefore be lacking in credibility. It would then be an inverse fantasy, a fairy tale of wickedness. However, this book is not proportionate in its structure. On the contrary, it is deliberately disparate. There are startling departures from its own predominant pattern of human conduct. It is precisely the deviation from the otherwise straight path of venom that gives this work a sense of reality. The incongruity of man affirms the truth of his existence.

---

[4] *Ibid.*, p. 76.

The breach of time between the narration and the events is the first obvious symbol of external dissonance. «Era una criatura y soy un viejo;...» In the description of outer reality the disparity is almost symbolically patterned in a perspective of inversion.

> ...su nombre era el del rey David y su apellido el de un fabricante de clavos que se llamaba Andrade...
> se llama Tomás de nombre, como el apóstol que dudó de la verdad, y Suárez de apellido, como su madre, que no recuerda el que tenía el padre...
> Tosió un poco con una tos ovejuna y con su bien timbrada y fina voz nos aseguró...
> ....me dijo que su nombre era Abraham y que el arco que en la mano llevaba era como el hambre, que hacía cantar las tripas, con el mérito, que el hambre no tenía...
> El señor alcalde, que tenía el corazón tan blando como duro el semblante..., comenzó mi ruina cuando cabía pensar que hubiera de ser el paso primero de la felicidad. [5]

If the inner structure of the book were also distinguishable by this monotonous rhythm of contrariety, *Nuevas Andanzas y Desventuras de Lazarillo de Tormes* would be at best an inferior version of a 17th-century picaresque novel bereft of judgment, presumed or well-intentioned. However, the characters' inner lives are not immured in antithetical emblems. Their actions are not confined to allegorical contrasts. In their freedom from disproportionate symbols, they follow an irregular pattern which does not rest on logical concepts but rather on their own personal possibilities, in varying degree logical and illogical but always singularly their own.

In contrast to the horror of hanging bodies and sausages, there are moments of pathos and inoffensive humor, instances of kind tears and harmless laughter. As in *La Familia de Pascual Duarte* pity creates an image of beauty.

> la señorita Marie parecía un ángel lleno de tristeza...
> ...el niño no es mío...
> —A éste no lo quiso porque nació cieguecito.
> Me cubrí la cara con las manos. Se me habían humedecido los ojos, no pude evitarlo. [6]

---

[5] *Ibid.*, pp. 59-60; 61; 62-63; 79.
[6] *Ibid.*, p. 147.

Humor, too, has its moment of purity.

> —¿Qué quiere cenar?
> —Lo que haya.
> —Aquí hay de todo, pida usted.
> —Pues déme vaca.
> —No, vaca no hay.
> —Pues unos huevos.
> —No, huevos no hay más que uno y es para mí.
> —Que le aproveche. ¿Hay patatas?
> —No, se han acabado.
> —Pues... déme lo que se estile, a mí me es igual.
> —Le daré cecina, ¿le gusta la cecina? [7]

But Lázaro does not remain in this state of quiescent felicity. Nor does he completely revert to apathetic horror. There are no limitations to his pattern of behavior in his search for material existence. He conforms to multitudinous situations and adjusts his manner of being to the lives of others. His own life is contained in the experiences of different characters. By virtue of being an active receptacle, he has a serpentine existence. For example, in order to gain admission to the home of don Federico, «el unico hombre que me pareció decente, y no me equivoqué»,[8] Lázaro relies on the poetic expressions of the good man.

> ...Nosotros hemos andado muchas leguas, señor, hemos visto altos chopos en el camino, frágiles cañas en los cañaverales, juncos que cimbrean a las orillas de las aguas que corren rumorosas; nosotros hemos oído, señor, silbar al mirlo desde la enramada... [9]

Lázaro's pragmatic transformations are not entirely vacuous. He becomes, at least in part, that which he is feigning to be, a poet as well as a thief. They are, naturally, temporary conversions; he is tinted with other forms but does not quite assume shape himself.

The course of Lázaro's life is determined by hunger. There are deviations, but the instinct for self-preservation prevails. There are pauses of good and evil but the pilgrimage toward satiation continues unabashed by moral considerations. The reader may infer judgment

---

[7] *Ibid.*, p. 183.
[8] *Ibid.*, p. 152.
[9] *Ibid.*, p. 161.

from Lázaro's piteous lamentations of his lot but the plaints, themselves, are inspired by self-interest. If Lázaro has a moral position, it is dictated by his sense of well-being. Therein lies much of the horror of the characterization of Lázaro, from whom we would presume to be different. Actually, he is identifiable with the world around us. Even as a caricature, Lázaro evokes the image of the «well-adjusted» man.

Although Lázaro lacks a sense of universal morality, he is not devoid of a consciouness of his being. First of all, he knows that he is fashioned after a 16th-century literary character.

> revolviendo una vez entre los papeles de un amo judío, boticario... me encontré cierto día con un libro que hablaba de un Lázaro de Tormes...
> ...me ilusiona pensar que aquel Lázaro fuera abuelo mío... [10]

Secondly, he has an awareness of the socio-political conditions that make possible the nature of his life. The picaresque novel gives him external identification; contemporary Spain gives him inner meaning. The outer composition of Lázaro recalls the 16th century; his vital fabric reflects Spanish life in the nineteen forties. Literature is his history, the realm of human experience his actuality.

It is the contemporaneity of his essential make-up, rather than his literary historicity, that sustains Lázaro's characterization of himself and his environment. It is further this sense of isochronism in events that lends force to the grotesqueness of Lázaro's peregrinatory existence. The revulsion that Lázaro inspires —and he is the most obnoxious of Cela's characters— occurs because his experiences are propinquous to the present, if not concurrent with it. More than his literary «grandfather» of the 16th century, this modern rogue seeks to encompass social totality, to be a crude representation of prevailing values and ideals. His birth as a literary character occurs after he has reflected on his sense of symbolic «open» reality.

Devoid of sophistication (even Pascual Duarte felt inhibited in his language, if not in his actions) Cela's picaresque protagonist is as exoteric in his observations as he is in his conduct. Thus, he serves as an effective prolocutor for the author. In this novel, Cela need

---

[10] *Ibid.*, pp. 33-34.

not resort to literary «tricks», such as the intrusive letters of *Pabellón de Reposo,* to manifest his intent. His attitude toward Spain is readily transmitted by the protagonist. Lázaro need not sacrifice his sense of reality while becoming Cela's vehicle of expression.

The retrospective account of the *pícaro* is expected to be unreserved in topic and style. It is not surprising, therefore, that he should project his personality in the experience of his milieu. The disparate nature of his life permits him to perceive all aspects of the world in which he lives, especially if they relate to his personal situation. He may recreate events which are remote from the reader's realm of possibility, or he may reveal perspectives which are not quite so anomalous. In the matter of the *pícaro's* vision of Spain, his view evokes a truth of horror precisely because it is very likely to be commensurate with that of people of flesh and blood, not excluding the author. The more our position may coincide —even momentarily— with that of this extra-social character, the more objectionable we find him. The greater the truth, the more incongruous the allegory.

One sentence in *Nuevas Andanzas y Desventuras de Lazarillo de Tormes* would suffice to discern the immanent cadence of Lázaro's march of hunger: «En España no hay ningún don Federico más».[11] Thus, even the literary existence of the poetic good man is effaced. Subsequent expressions are basically anti-climactic though elucidatory.

> A mis plantas se veían los pueblos colocados como con la mano, y antes de decidirme por cuál habría de ser el mío, los contemplé con calma, como el señor de todos, regodeándome en imaginarlos fértiles y acogedores como, por desgracia mía, ninguno de ellos era, y ordenados y ricos como, para desgracia de sus moradores, ni uno solo resultó.
> Miré para el levante y vi poblachos en ruinas y aldehuelas miserables de hermosos nombres.[12]

Dried blood stresses the nature of the blurred view. «...miré otra vez para el letrero y pude ver que la almagra ya tenía —de puro vieja— el rojo y como entristecido color de la sangre seca.»[13] The world of Lázaro seems reduced to a lifeless skeleton; it lacks the

---

[11] *Ibid.,* p. 177.
[12] *Ibid.,* p. 179.
[13] *Ibid.,* p. 181.

vitality of flowing blood. Its horror is rancid.[14] Life is virtually decomposed.

While Cela's role as a «puppeteer» is patent in Lázaro's cynical commentary on Spain, the picaresque protagonist does assume in his creation the stature of literary independence. Were it not for these explosive affirmations of unparalleled individuality, the characterization of Lázaro would be reduced to that of a «puppet» and the book might become a didactic dramatic essay. However, Cela's attitude toward his country must be evaluated not only in terms of the «thesis» aspect of the novel, but also in the realm of creation. It is in the manifestation of independent artistic entities that the author, willingly or not, will reveal his innermost feelings toward the world in which he lives. Thus, Lázaro will express as much of Cela, if not more, in his behavior as an integer, as he will as a prolocutor. As a mouthpiece Lázaro represents traditional picaresque negation, as a unique literary character he is not so simple to decipher. His utterances of abomination, which identify his exterior, are tempered by a surreptious feeling of sympathy for the weaknesses of humanity. There is, in effect, disproportion in the structure of Lázaro. Although the sense of harsh external reality prevails, it is not completely unilateral. Intermingled with the predominant odor of rancidness occasionally is the weak fragrance of wine. The result is not entirely palatable, but it makes the odor bearable.

For the most part Lázaro follows the path of the *pícaro*, relentless in his own material pursuit of happiness. Contained in the lives of others, he appears to have no inner life of his own. At infrequent intervals, however, he frees himself from the enslavement of his circumstances —and from the control of the author— to emerge as an unpredictable literary person, a real novelistic character. His ironic evaluation of himself in one case recalls Don Quijote's comment on the generosity of St. Martin,[15] «—Llegué a repartir cerca de una

---

[14] «Entré, y un olor a rancio me dió en las narices. Nada se veía en todo el vasto zaguán fuera del rincón que alumbraba el ventanillo... Pasó algún tiempo, volví yo a las voces y el niño al llanto, y por la escalera, que crujía y se quejaba como un desvanecido.» *Ibid.*, p. 182.

[15] «Descubrióla el hombre, y pareció ser la de San Martín puesto a caballo, que partía la capa con el pobre; y apenas lo hubo visto don Quijote, cuando dijo:

—Este caballero también fué de los aventureros cristianos, y creo que fué más liberal que valiente, como lo puedes echar de ver, Sancho, en que está

peseta, y más hubiera dado de haberme sobrado más,...» [16] Further observations of sympathetic irony are revealed when Lázaro transcending the plane of selfish misfortune speaks with piercing compassion of the two persons he loves, don Federico and la señorita Marie.

> ...don Federico me dió, con su saludo y con su «Dios te guarde», la puñalada de misericordia...
> ...le entró la vocación y se metió monja. La pobre fue lo mejor que pudo hacer. [17]

Without completely surrendering his essential captiousness, Cela's *pícaro* assumes a new dimension. Permeated with sympathy, his cynicism becomes humorous, his outlook more understanding. In his affection for others and in his ability to laugh at himself, Lázaro frees himself from the literary bondage into which he is born.

In his death or disappearance as a novelistic character, Lázaro also rises to Quixotic heights. His existence is peregrinatory. When his wanderings cease, his being is no more; his light of life is extinguished: «se apagó una vela cuando dejó de caminar». [18] His nemesis, as was Don Quijote's, is the large city. It is in Madrid where Lázaro suffers his most crushing defeat. In the capital the *pícaro* is incarcerated and made to submit to law and social order. Madrid is the cage.

> ¡Allí acabó mi libertad! Madrid, donde me las prometía tan felices, me metió en el cuartel, y en él, aunque a los dos meses escasos me sacó de asistente el teniente Díaz, me encontraba al principio como pienso que han de encontrarse los mirlos y los jilgueros al llegar a la jaula. [19]

The preceding passage is not only the description of Lázaro's uttermost frustration, but also the introduction to Cela's subsequent nov-

---

partiendo la capa con el pobre, y le da la mitad; y sin duda debía de ser entonces invierno; que si no, él se la diera toda, según era de caritativo.» Cervantes, *Don Quijote de la Mancha*, Parte Segunda, capítulo LVIII, pp. 49-50. Clásicos Castellanos, Vol. VIII, Edición y notas de Francisco Rodríguez Marín, Espasa-Calpe, Madrid, 1944.

[16] *Ibid.*, p. 172.
[17] *Ibid.*, p. 165.
[18] *Ibid.*, p. 260.
[19] *Ibid.*, p. 250.

el, *La Colmena*. In the last two pages of *Nuevas Andanzas y Desventuras de Lazarillo de Tormes* we have already the precursory movement, a sort of musical prologue for *La Colmena*. The effect of Madrid is further clarified.

> Cuando al cabo del tiempo me licenciaron, tenía todo: una documentación, una cartilla, un certificado de buena conducta... Lo único que me faltaba eran las ganas de seguir caminando sin ton ni son... [20]

Here we have a climate that destroys the will to be. The city saps man's strength and transmogrifies him into a molecule. So Lázaro, who might now transmigrate, at least peripherally, into one of the many characters of *La Colmena* comes to the realization that human life is purposelessly microcosmatic.

> Después... conocí días felices y semanas desgraciadas; gocé la buena salud y padecí el hambre...
> Contar el camino, ¿para qué? Fue la espinosa senda de todos quienes conocí.. [21]

---

[20] *Ibid.*, p. 251.
[21] *Ibid.*, p. 251.

V. LA COLMENA

La Colmena (1951) represents the highest point of Cela's literary career. Possibly, not since the appearance of Benito Pérez Galdós' *Fortunata y Jacinta* (1886-1887) has there been such a dramatic recreation of Hispanic life in novel form.[1] *La Colmena*, in its consideration of merely three days of human existence in Madrid, penetrates the inner core of centuries of Spanish civilization. Its external preoccupation is with the ephemeral, Madrid in the early nineteen forties; in its inner structure it reveals the meaning of a way of life which is, for better or for worse, singularly and irreducibly Spanish. The fragmentary presentation intones the theme of disintegration, «el vivir desviviéndose».[2] Yet, however difficult, however destructive, however incongruous, the emphasis is on *vivir*.

The ominous physical reality of hunger pervades the scene. It serves as a motivating force for external behavior. It is horrible. It is real. But hunger is fundamentally the literary pretext in *La Colmena*. The inner experiences of the characters, their immanent conflicts, transcend material contemplation. In spite of their similarities with contemporary counterparts of flesh and blood, Cela's literary persons have a durable intimate existence which is tangibly artistic. Their lives are worth creating and experiencing not because they may be imaginary «case studies», but because they enclose within their personal exterior an agonizing existence which is essentially that of Spain—and possibly of

---

[1] Although Cela's display of arrogance tends to alienate critics, we must strive to be objective and judge Cela's art in spite of himself. «Me considero el más importante novelista español desde el 98, y me espanta el considerar lo fácil que me resultó. Pido perdón por no haberlo podido evitar». Camilo José Cela, *Baraja de Invenciones*, Editorial Castalia, Valencia, 1953, p. 8, «Breve Autobiografía del Inventor».

[2] See note 32 chapter II.

all humanity. Quite naturally, the inner meaning of their lives was not perceived by the censors, who, in their paleolithic role, forbade the publication of this book in Spain.

That *La Colmena* should inspire shame in its portrayal of living history is entirely comprehensible. No nation views its penury with pride. Nor does Cela manifest satisfaction with the Hell of hunger that was Spain after the Civil War. On the contrary, he cries with grief.[3] As he creates, he feels the torture of his people, the anguish of Spain. Nonetheless, Cela's vision is not peripheral; he sees beyond matter, and beyond the circumstantial state of man. He avails himself of transitory material truth to penetrate the intra-historical significance of Spanish life. The outer reality of *La Colmena*, the plight of Spain in the early nineteen forties, so shocking to the pride of censors, is a mutable circumstance (indeed, with the help of the United States it has changed considerably in 20 years). What remains constant is the artisitc expression of a way of life which is integrally Spanish.

If hunger were viewed as causation in a behavioristic fashion, *La Colmena* would become a psycho-economic treatise on human conduct. And if it is that, too, it is also much more. The author is conscious of the havoc that hunger causes. But hunger is often a disguise, an apology for human actions, and Cela is intent on «unmasking life».[4] The depiction of social conditions in itself is not conducive to an appreciation of Cela's unmasked image of Spain. Beyond the external circumstances, which constitute the scenery of their lives, their orbit, stand the characters in their unshrouded reality. In their reaction to hunger, and other prevailing conditions, in their suffering they reveal themselves. And as they lay bare their souls, they disclose their creator's conception of the world which they and he share—Spain.

In spite of the persistent horror of hunger which permeates the existence of the characters, *La Colmena* expresses a vision of Spain which is intimately sympathetic. In a fragmentary fashion, sympathy

---

[3] See note 1, chapter I. His revenge is also his revenge on himself for being Spanish.

[4] «Mienten quienes quieren disfrazar la vida con la máscara loca de la literatura. Ese mal que corroe las almas; ese mal que tiene tantos nombres como queramos darle, no puede ser combatido con los paños calientes del conformismo, con la cataplasma de la retórica y de la poética.» Camilo José Cela, *La Colmena,* Editorial Noguer, S. A., Barcelona, octubre de 1955, «Nota a la Primera Edición».

prevails in the creation of characters.⁵ Although externally it may be unbelievably appalling to the well-fed Anglo-Saxon world, and definitely unpalatable to the Spaniards who do not wish to be reminded of the circumstances of the nineteen forties, the recreation of life in Madrid is motivated by love. It is not a unidimensional feeling which can be translated in terms of *approval* or *admiration*. By no means. Especially on the part of Cela it is a complex attitude which is fundamentally disproportionate in its rhapsodical content. It is filled with grief and despair; it has no purpose other than to embrace the agony of living; it is incongruous, self-contradictory; it is «a voice in the desert».⁶ Often it is ambivalent, adulterated (or perhaps so it is purified) with hatred, but it is love, the love for Spanish life which guides the pen of Cela in *La Colmena*. The author struggles with the external prevailing structure of his civilization, but he surrenders to its inner foundation. For all his avowed intention to narrate «a slice of life without charity»,⁷ his pen gains independence and intuitively it becomes profoundly charitable.

Although superficially *La Colmena* presents a panorama of human abjection with overtones of opprobrium, there is not a single character, of the more than three hundred who appear in this work,⁸ who evokes unmixed horror. Even the most cruelly repulsive ones, such as the sodomists, also inspire pity. The formula is not always rationally discernible; nor is it invariable. The blend is often crude. Nonetheless, its effect is perspicuous. Whereas in the three earlier novels *rejection* was the catalytic agent which established the rapport between the reader and the characters, here the bond is magnetic attraction. Logically,

---

⁵ By *sympathy* I mean the bonds that vitally link the begetter and the creatures begotten.

⁶ «Sé bien que *La Colmena* es un grito en el desierto;... un grito no demasiado estridente o desgarrador.» *Op. Cit.*, «Nota a Esta Segunda Edición».

⁷ «Esta novela mía no aspira a ser más —ni menos, ciertamente— que un trozo de vida narrada pasa a paso, sin reticencias, sin extrañas tragedias, *sin caridad*, como la vida discurre, exactamente como la vida discurre.» *Ibid.*, «Nota a la Primera Edición». (The italics are mine.)

⁸ Cela had counted only one hundred and sixty but the publisher points out that the author has been too modest. «N. del E. — Se trata de un cálculo muy modesto por parte del autor; en el censo que figura en el presente volumen, José Manuel Caballero Bonald recuenta doscientos noventa y seis personajes imaginarios y cincuenta personajes reales: en total, trescientos cuarenta y seis.» *Ibid.*, «Nota a la Primera Edición».

one may maintain the position of revulsion; artistically, one is charmed, as if by enchantment, into a state of compenetration. The bond of sympathy that exists between the author and his literary persons flows into the reader and radiates magic participation.

Unlike its literary «stepfather», [9] *Fortunata y Jacinta*, the most significant Spanish novel of the 19th century, which touches upon all strata of Madrid society, *La Colmena* centers its attention on one *café*. Here is focused the languishing existence of human lives whose destinies are interwoven by hunger. The habitués, many of whom are extra-social, constitute a gallery of distinctive individuals who appear to be no more than a mass of humanity when viewed panoramically. Their uniqueness, their anchoritic existence, is revealed as the book progresses and the characters are examined microscopically not only in relation to the other characters but also in relation to themselves. Thus, the *café* of doña Rosa reaches out with its tentacles and penetrates into the inner recesses of hundreds of literary persons, who are directly or indirectly bound to this establishment. Sometimes the chain that shackles the people to their places in the *café* seems unanchored, but their purposeless life knows no other course. In the world of *Fortunata y Jacinta* man was in conflict with his destiny; in the world of *La Colmena* he hasn't even discovered what his destiny is. [10]

La Colmena is in a sense, the sub-title of the book which is denominated as the beginning of a series, *Caminos inciertos*. In this beehive of humanity there is no gathering of honey. The convocation of drifting lives has no organization; there are no certain roads. Some of

---

[9] In my opinion there is no direct literary relationship between Cela and Galdós. Many writers have dedicated themselves to expressing in novelistic form their vision of Spain. That Galdós and Cela should have succeeded in forging literary masterpieces in their recreation of Spanish life is a coincidence of genius.

[10] In spite of the various logical meanings of *destino*, the stylistic meaning coincides with the meaning of *destiny*. «Ahora anda buscando un destino, pero no lo encuentra... El joven poeta está componiendo un poema largo, que se llama 'Destino'. Tuvo sus dudas sobre si debía poner 'El destino', pero al final, y después de consultar con algunos poetas ya más hechos, pensó que no, que sería mejor titularlo 'Destino', simplemente. Era más sencillo, más evocador, más misterioso. Además así, llamándole 'Destino', quedaba más sugeridor, más... ¿cómo diríamos?, más impreciso, más poético. Así no se sabía si quería aludir a 'el destino', o a 'un destino', a 'destino incierto', a 'destino fatal' o 'destino feliz' o 'destino azul' o 'destino violado'. 'El destino' ataba más, dejaba menos campo para que la imaginación volase en libertad, desligada de toda traba.» *Op. Cit.*, pages 19 and 25.

the inhabitants pretend to be searching for identity; the majority doesn't even bother. Their motions are habitual as though they were mechanically operated. Thus, they all appear to be playing their roles in life fatalistically with the complete submission to the historical circumstances of their time. This is the phantasmagoria of *La Colmena,* its stage effect.

A more penetrating perspective of the scene, an examination of the individual characters in their intimate surroundings, reveals underneath the aimlessness of their lives a world of personal agonizing frustration. Indeed, the conflict is not well-defined; sometimes it is merely the struggle of living, but it is experienced with fierce intensity. As they strive to express themselves, not quite knowing how or why, they suffer in their uncertainty. In their nebulous ties with historical values, especially the Hispanic sense of honor, they manifest a disproportionate existence which does not seem to fit any ideal pattern. They are not prepared to confront ancient images iconoclastically; nor can they afford the luxury of revering them. While the cruel reality of an empty stomach does not completely reduce them to animals, it does in part divest them of the halo of civilization. This is their struggle, to maintain an aura of civilization while physically being reduced to animalism.

The battle is patrimonially instinctive. There is a vestige of intuitive historicity. In spite of their material vicissitudes, the characters feel the need to preserve their personal dignity. Even Elvirita, the prostitute, has her pride! [11] Often the façade of civilization has its pitiably ludicrous moments, but for all its misdirection and senseless incongruity, it is expressed sympathetically. The most horribly ridiculous situations do not detract from the compassion that the characters inspire. Horror does not efface pity; on the contrary, in this novel the brutal reality of the physical world lends force to the understanding of equivocal lives which have «uncertain roads».

The descriptive fragmentation of individual existences does not break the spell of sympathy. As the account of one life evaporates, there is no vacuum; it flows into the narration of another. There is an arabesque continuity with no definite beginning and certainly no end.

---

[11] «—¿Por qué no se arregla con don Pablo? —Porque no quiero. Una también tiene su orgullo, doña Rosa... La señorita Elvira se mostró digna y suspicaz.» *Op. Cit.,* pp. 28-29 and 49.

If there is no one protagonist, neither is there an antagonist, unless both be contained within the persons as in marriage. The stories proceed in all directions; some lives are recaptured, others evanesce. The thread of the narration is as irregular as the histories it retells. Incidents which at first are easily forgotten as they are replaced by others return to haunt us. Often what appeared to be insignificant is revealed with its profound fire of human hatred and love. Sometimes apparent irrelevances remain suppressed along with what seemed to be great events. The sensation is erratic. One cannot discriminate in his remembrances or his forgetfulness. The vision is overwhelming; it defies the reader's acumen. One's judgment is crushed. There only remains the impression of pity transcending horror.

The moribund atmosphere of Madrid exorcises specters of human depravation but they are transitory impressions. Impossible dreams and hopeless illusions, on the other hand, survive the tide of evanescence. Their evocative despair creates a sensation of greater reality than all the physical acts. The particular events are soon forgotten, perhaps the particular illusions, too. What endures is the grievous image of the hopeless dreams, the truth of their impossible aspirations.

In the picaresque setting of Cela's *Nuevas Andanzas y Desventuras de Lazarillo de Tormes* there were no dreams, only nightmares. In *La Colmena* man may not know what his longing should be, but often he yearns for another sphere of identity. Thus, the young bootblack happily seeks to affiliate himself with don Leonardo, a man of fine appearance, who has robbed the boy of his savings.[12] The reality of his dream surpasses material catastrophies. The association with what he considers another social class is worth the sacrifice of his wealth, accrued in self-abnegation. Dreams are the stuff that men are made of in this novel. The myth of the *señor* persists: «—Los señores son los señores, está más claro que el agua».[13]

Petrita, the servant, doesn't consider herself worthy of Martín Marco's affection. A starving poet, he is in another class by virtue of being the brother of her mistress. In her expression of selfless love, she submits to personal sacrifice in order to preserve the magic of her

---

[12] «El limpia siente admiración por don Leonardo. El que don Leonardo le haya robado sus ahorros es, por lo visto, algo que le llena de pasmo y de lealtad...» *Op. Cit.*, p. 41.

[13] *Ibid.*, p. 68.

dream. But to reveal herself to her idol would be to break the spell of her illusions.

>—Oiga, ¿yo valgo veintidós pesetas?...
>—Cóbrese usted los cafés del señorito Martín...
>—¿Y tú por qué haces esto por el señorito Martín?
>—Pues porque me da la gana y porque lo quiero más que a nada en el mundo; a todo el que lo quiera saber se lo digo, a mi novio el primero.
>Petrita, con las mejillas arreboladas, el pecho palpitante, la voz ronca, el pelo en desorden y los ojos llenos de brillo, tenía una belleza extraña, como de leona recién casada.
>—¿Y él te corresponde?
>—No le dejo. [14]

Twenty-two *pesetas* is the exact change that Martín Marco is receiving at that moment after paying his bill at a *café*.

In the assemblage of heterogenous personages there are those who dream very little. These are the practical people who thrive on the hunger of others. They are «realistic» in their adjustment to social conditions. Their success has the universal quality of cruelty expressed through self-preservation. The reality of these characters rests on the «true to life» fabric of ephemerality. They constitute the background of apathetic familiarity. Their banal identity, tangibly recognizable, is cast into oblivion. They are neither hated nor loved. In the process of artistic disintegration they disappear, leaving in their wake no imaginative sphere to perpetuate their existence. Their literary fate is their punishment, the author's revenge on his society.

The ordinary displays of cruelty on the part of doña Rosa are innocuously archaeological in substance. They interrupt but they do not affect the uncertain course of human lives. Along with other thriving business magnates like the uncouth don Mario de la Vega, the wealthy printer, and doña Ramona Bragado, the usurious procuress, doña Rosa forms part of the dramatic chorus. They are all crude representations of the realm of human experience. They appear to be photographed rather than painted. They are the «facts» of the Spanish way of life, the stage for the tragedy. Without them there is no theatre. They may be facsimiles, but they are indispensable for the performance.

---

[14] *Ibid.*, pp. 148-49.

Although outwardly at the beginning all characters seem to be stage props, carbon copies of life, as the narration ensues introspectively beyond the scenography of the novel there is revealed before us a host of undecipherable lives struggling to exist outside of their circumscribed social limits. The vision lacks the perspective of proportion. It is fragmentary, at times virtually undeveloped, embryonic in its form. But it is sustained by sympathy and by means of this pillar it lives. In *La Colmena* the story is not completed. The events are left as if in suspended animation; so is the development of characters. What remains is the substance that links the author and the reader to the unfinished novelistic symphony—vital sympathy.

La Colmena lacks the historical continuity of the genre to be considered a traditional novel. Its disproportionate form reflects the incongruity of its content, its schism with the past. The era which Cela is recreating represents a radical departure from chronological order. Ontologically the epoch is the deformed product of chaos, an abortion of history. Its course is no more clear, «caminos inciertos». The meaning of life is no longer contained in explicit ideals. And yet, man continues to dream amidst the rubbles of human decay. This in essence is the novel of *La Colmena*. But it is more. As it captures the reality of illusions, it penetrates within the foundation of the Spanish way of life, with its contradictory irrational beauty. In its fragmentary analysis of contemporary chaotic life, Cela presents a living history of a people whose agonizing personal existence surmounts physical calamities. The real continuity of the novel rests on the projection of human lives who constitute the chain of actual history. Before one man's story is extinguished, another has begun.

The effect of this novel is a logical consequence of the deliberate novelistic technique. There is a sensation of overwhelming anonymity in the never ending incomplete personal images. The intent of the artist, to create explosive fragments of related partial lives is achieved. The approach is itself a reflection of the author's conscious experience of his society. There predominates in his art a perspective of life propelled by aimless distortive obliteration. But in the inexorable course of becoming ashes and dust life is illumined and we are infected with its vitality rather than its imperfect finality.

Immured in an abyss of degradation, gnawed by famine, human existence fulminates in unconformable ascendancy. The movement from the mire of despair lacks cohesion. It defies the logical confinement of patterns. It asserts itself in unpredictable moments. Sometimes it perishes in descent, as it is absorbed by the composition of its incarceration. In any case, in its rise or in its fall, the evanescent fulfillment of life is alluring in the atmosphere of eventual overwhelming destruction. The integration of man and his circumstances surpasses consideration of cause and effect. Within this valley of attrition man maps his own course of submission or resistance, adjustment or opposition. In action or inaction, in self-determination or in apathy, the path of one life affects the passage of another. The journey is trajectory as human lives traverse one another.

The kindling quality of individual experiences, the ability that unknowingly one life has to incite the fire of apparent unrelated human existence, evokes wonderment and admiration. The interactive juxtaposition of atomic experiences is neither fortuitous nor romantically coincidental. It is the collection of distinct entities that constitute the whole, and at no time is the whole more significant than any of its parts. The most socially unworthy resident of Madrid may spark a chain reaction of events that could affect the total composition of mankind in that city. The vision is personalistic. The strength of life, consciously or unconsciously, lies within the person himself. He may be victimized by the conditions that surround his birth, but he is not wrested of his innate endowment to affirm himself and exert vital influence in vanquishment as in triumph, in degradation as in exaltation. This is the living truth of *La Colmena*. In its perpetual driftway, life is vitally radiating.

Distilled in a shapeless moment of history, traditional Hispanic values are anomalously contained in the experiences of *La Colmena*. The myth of the *señor,* the concept of honor, the reverence of masculinity are expressed in varying degrees. As clothing of appearance seldom do they fit. In most cases they are worn in a pattern of horror and humor, but sporadically, as if by accident, there is an occasional semblance of harmony. In the crumbling cave that is Madrid not all succumb insensibly to the lava around them. In some cases, and these are the literary persons by whom we are most affected, human dignity prevails. For example, Victorita, who is about to become the victim of circumstances, disarms her tormentors with her frankness.

> —No, doña Ramona. No tengo tiempo. Me espera mi novio. A mí, ¿sabe usted?, ya me revienta andar dándole vueltas al asunto, como un borrico de noria. Mire usted, a usted y a mí lo que nos interesa es ir al grano, ¿me entiende?
> —No, hija, no te entiendo.
> Victorita tenía el pelo algo revuelto.
> —Pues se lo voy a decir más claro: ¿dónde está el cabrito?...
> —Por mí, sí. Por seis mil duros soy capaz de pasarme toda la vida obedeciéndole a usted. ¡Y más vidas que tuviera! [15]

It is she who becomes the master of her agonizing situation: «ella sabía muy bien dónde se metía».[16] In apparent submission to hunger, the victim confronts herself with her destiny whereas the merchants of despair are in reality the ones who become the slaves of their good fortune. They know no other course. Victorita struggles with herself before and while fulfilling her decision. But, like Areusa in *La Celestina*, it is she who wills her conflict. Her tubercular fiancé, the object of her inmolation, remains apathetic. He is the helpless inciting force, the spiritless reason for her actions.

For the most part, the characters of *La Colmena*, especially the men, are sympathetically passive. They are often unaware of their radiating vigor. It is among the women that we find the most novelistically impressive protagonists. The virility of men is expressed primarily as a socially outmoded role, the fulfillment of femeninity is asserted willfully, sometimes submissively, but occasionally defiantly. Thus, when don Roque and Julita, father and daughter, recognize each other in the stairway of Celia's house, a rendezvous for lovers, it is the daughter who is the tragic character, the one who has brought about her fate. The father is the pathetic one. Immersed in his male role, his presence in this house is predetermined. Julita, on the contrary, is the socially unexpected visitor. Of course, they are both surprised to see each other, momentarily stunned. In due time, however, it will be Julita's life which will be affected by her determination to be extra-social; her father will continue to play his role with little feeling other than paternal sorrow for his daughter.

---

[15] *Ibid.*, pp. 246 and 232.
[16] *Ibid.*, p. 171.

In the turmoil of Madrid life, there is a curious clarity about the structure of domesticity. The external semblance of masculine rule is ummasked. The female is the dominant creature. This is quite clear in the case of the baker, el señor Ramón, who is ensnared in the disguise of legendary tradition. He must pretend to be the master of his household.

> El señor Ramón se queda un momento callado. Se rasca la cabeza y baja la voz.
> —No le diga nada a la Paulina...
> —Descuide...
> —No es por nada, ¿sabe? Yo sé que es usted un hombre discreto que no se va de la lengua, pero a lo mejor, por un casual, se le escapaba a usted algo y ya teníamos monserga para quince días. Aquí mando yo, como usted sabe, pero las mujeres ya las conoce usted... [17]

The role of the baker is pungently explicit. It is not observed as a phenomenon, but rather as a patrimonial expression of patriarchal origin.

> Su biografía es una biografía de cinco líneas. Llegó a la capital a los ocho o diez años, se colocó en una tahona y estuvo ahorrando hasta los veintiuno, que fue al servicio. Desde que llegó a la ciudad hasta que se fue quinto no gastó ni un céntimo, lo guardó todo. Comió pan y bebió agua, durmió debajo del mostrador y no conoció mujer. Cuando se fue a servir al Rey dejó sus cuartos en la Caja Postal y, cuando lo licenciaron, retiró su dinero y se compró una panadería; en doce años había ahorrado veinticuatro mil reales, todo lo que ganó: algo más de una peseta diaria, unos tiempos con otros. En el servicio aprendió a leer, a escribir y a sumar, y perdió la inocencia. Abrió la tahona, se casó, tuvo doce hijos, compró un calendario y se sentó a ver pasar el tiempo. Los patriarcas antiguos debieron ser bastante parecidos al señor Ramón. [18]

In the account of the merchant's banal life the author punctures the legendary balloons of history. By means of irony, with profound sympathy for the halucinatory male ego, the novelist brings down myths to the realm of human experience. The reader smiles with feeling

---

[17] *Ibid.*, p. 79.
[18] *Ibid.*, p. 80.

at *el señor* Ramón and if he is a male also at himself. There is no acrimony in this penetrating perspective of Hispanic values. The vision does not imply judgment, other than understanding for the vacuum of social beliefs. The baker's illusory role gives him a dimension of sympathy which the non-dreamers lack. By his dilusions *el señor* Ramón establishes a core of identity with the flesh and blood reader.

The impetuous sense of honor is humorously tempered by reason. La señora de Cazuela anticipates death at the hand of her husband, don Fernando, when her adulterous transgression is uncovered. Don Fernando, whose *don* would hardly fit the ancient concept of dignity, aware of the presence of the police who are investigating a possible murder in the building, assumes a rational position before the personal offense.

> —¡Ay, Fernando! ¡Mátame si quieres! Pero que nuestro hijito no se entere de nada.
> —No, hija, ¡cómo te voy a matar con el juzgado en casa! Anda, vete a la cama. ¡Lo único que nos faltaba ahora es que tu querido resultase el asesino de doña Margot! [19]

Don Fernando's attitude, self-derisive in nature, suggests decadent horror. The comical aspect is the cruel instrument of destruction as the breach is made with the past. Again, the fable of tradition is distorted. In his extreme reasonable position don Fernando appears ill-proportioned, as it were, insanely logical. Yet he is not nearly so ill-formed in appearance as the anachronistic consuetudes. It is the outmoded convention of honor that seems ridiculous. If there is ironic wrath, it is not directed against the individual but rather against society. Don Fernando makes us laugh, but it is not at him that we laugh. When the individual discards the concept of honor he is not so ridiculous as when he attempts to adapt it to his own particular concept of comfort. —¡Si por lo menos se hubiera ido de Madrid!— decía su hermano Paco, que tenía un concepto geográfico del honor.» [20]

In his recreation of Madrid life Cela penetrates the most recondite recesses of intimate existence. In the tradition of Galdós, whose

---

[19] *Ibid.*, p. 133.
[20] *Ibid.*, p. 277.

vision of a honeymoon was masterfully described in the early pages of *Fortunata y Jacinta,* Cela delicately depicts the nuptial bliss of *los* González, parents of five children. Not all interesting characters in *La Colmena* are extra-social. The personal struggles are not gigantic in all cases. The trivialities of daily life also constitute a source for novelistic situations. For example, Roberto González upon receiving an advance on his salary from don Ramón, the baker, sees an indigent child of six years of age. The child is collecting a few pennies and some olives that have been thrown on the ground from the nearby tavern. Don Roberto behaves in the novelistic fashion of Galdós' Torquemada in *Torquemada en la Hoguera.*

> Don Roberto cierra el tragaluz y se queda de pie en medio de la habitación. Estuvo pensando en llamar al niño y darle un real.
> —No...
> A don Roberto, al imponerse el buen sentido, le volvió el optimismo. [21]

Don Roberto González is a kind man, but he is not absolute in his virtues. Often his common sense guides his life. Don Roberto González expresses the inadequacy of abstract values when the values conflict with self-interest. Don Roberto González reminds us of ourselves.

Remarkably free of concupiscence, *La Colmena* explores the nether regions of Madrid as well as bourgeois life. In the revolving existence of the Spanish capital there is a common denominator of intermingling experiences which relate all classes of society to a mutual chain of events. The *café* is the primary focal point, the axis. Its relentless rotation is diffusive. It creates lesser zones of convergence, the home, the business establishment, the brothel. In all cases, the recreation of life is sympathetic. Human experiences are as tenderly depicted free of conventional moral judgment in one place as in another. In all instances the emphasis is on the person, not on his type of dwelling. Regardless of his profession or social standing a character may be pos-

---

[21] *Ibid.,* pp. 82-83. This incident recalls how Torquemada reacts to his desire to be kind. «...'Señor, señor —decía con el temblor de un frío intenso— mire cómo estoy, míreme.' Torquemada pasó de largo y se detuvo a poca distancia, volvió hacia atrás, estuvo un rato vacilando, y al fin siguió su camino. En el cerebro le fulguró esta idea: 'Si conforme traigo la capa nueva, trajera la vieja...'» *Torquemada en la Hoguera,* pp. 54-55.

sessed of lust or he may be virtuous, or both. Perhaps the salient aspect of this humane attitude is the unexpected expression of goodness on the part of the extra-social people in this novel. But there is no generic classification of virtue and sin. They are not qualities that are identifiable with a given class or position; nor do they have fixed residence in their one person. There is no constancy about them. They are migratory in nature. Doña Ramona Bragado, an amateur procuress, who operates within a semblance of respectability, appears as a cruel merchant of despair in the moments that we see her. Doña Jesusa, the professional *Celestina,* on the other hand, reveals herself as a kind person, quite uncommercial in nature in the photographic glimpse we have of her. Similarly, Pura, whose name seems to belie her profession, in unison with Martín Marco reaches unpredictable novelistic heights in transcending her assigned role. «Se durmieron en un abrazo como dos recién casados.» [22] Free of lasciviousness and free of sentimentality the house of iniquity is just another junction for the expression of human lives. Momentarily it may sow seeds of grace. Doña Jesusa and Pura will no doubt revert to a mercenary position, proper of their vocation, but there will be unforeseen deviations. Their lives are not orderly; they do not fit social patterns of codification other than in their external figure.

Just as the citadel of peccancy may permit within its ugly walls the presence of virtue, so the expression of charity may enclose within its format a malevolent proclivity for sin. Doña Rosa, the owner of the *café,* does not even attain this degree of perversion. She prefers to be cruel in the security of her domicile.

> Al camarero le da un repel*u*co por el espinazo. Si fuese un hombre decidido hubiera ahogado a la dueña; afortunadamente no lo es. La dueña se ríe por lo bajo con una risita cruel. Hay gentes a las que divierte ver pasar calamidades a los demás; para verlas bien de cerca se dedican a visitar los barrios miserables, a hacer regalos viejos a los moribundos, a los tísicos arrumbados en una manta astrosa, a los niños anémicos y panzudos que tienen los huesos blandos, a las niñas que son madres a los once años, a las golfas cuarentonas comidas de bubas: las golfas que parecen caciques indios con sarna. Doña Rosa no llega ni a esa catego-

---

[22] *Ibid.,* p. 255.

ría. Doña Rosa prefiere la emoción a domicilio, ese temblor...[23]

A more civilized form of savagery would have been for doña Rosa to be professionally charitable. But the truculent business woman lacks imagination. She is practical; she has no illusory ambition, no lofty ideals, not even in the perverted form of social charity.

The derision of «applied» charity reaches out beyond the confines of the space and time of *La Colmena*. The critical references to the particular setting of the novel are usually more subtle. Mostly they are contained in the living experiences of the characters though there are dramatic incarnations of implied lamentations. The six years old child who screams a song in a shrieking voice, hoping to receive alms in his attempt to survive, represents the chorus of despair.[24] Reappearing throughout the narration, his hunger is pathetically symbolical. A more penetrating display of pathos is contained in the experiences of doña Celia's grand nephews, who eagerly await the arrival of couples because their illicit presence means a hot meal the following day.

> Los niños, cuando llega alguna pareja, gritan jubilosos por el pasillo: '¡Viva, viva, que ha venido otro señor!' Los angelitos saben que el que entre un señor con una señorita del brazo, significa comer caliente al otro día.[25]

La Colmena manifests only incidentally an anti-government attitude. The prevailing regime is dismissed scornfully as unworthy of much attention. Yet, there is an element of mockery in the occasional concrete references.

> —Los obreros —piensa— también tienen que comer, aunque muchos son tan rojos que no se merecerían tanto desvelo.
> ... como tenía un fondo patriótico, esperaban que fuese patrocinado por las autoridades.
> Su marido, don Obdulio Cortés López, del comercio, había muerto después de la guerra, a consecuencia, según

---

[23] *Ibid.*, p. 81.
[24] «El niño no tiene cara de persona, tiene cara de animal doméstico, de sucia bestia, de pervertida bestia de corral. Son muy pocos sus años para que el dolor haya marcado aún el navajazo del cinismo —o de la resignación— en su cara,...» *Ibid.*, p. 91.
[25] *Ibid.*, pp. 180-181.

> decía la esquela del ABC, de los padecimientos sufridos durante el dominio rojo.
>
> Los hermanos viven solos. Al padre lo fusilaron, por esas cosas que pasan, y la madre murió tísica y desnutrida el año 41. [26]

The *según decía* of the next to the last cited quotation inverts the logical exposition of the claim. It is sufficient to distort the allegation of the regime. A more wounding reference is the episode of the parrot, who is about to be denounced by a super-patriot to the authorities. It appears that the parrot lacks the proper respect for the Church and for the government. He is an unquestionable heretic.

> ... el loro del segundo decía pecados.
> —Mira, Roque, esto ya no se puede aguantar. Si ese loro no se corrige, yo lo denuncio.
> —Pero, hija, ¿tú te das cuenta del choteo que se iba a organizar en la Comisaría cuando te viesen llegar para denunciar a un loro? [27]

This incident epitomizes the absurdity of the totalitarian situation. The problem of identification and continual governmental inspection is more serious, even if equally ridiculous. Thus, as the last pages of the book approach, Martín Marco unwittingly finds himself in great trouble. His papers are not in order.

By far, more agonizing to the author than the amenities of governmental regimentation is the animalistic attitude of the people who surrender in spirit and are amalgamated into a state of being a flattering flock. They are sycophants. They will do anything in order to ingratiate themselves with the powerful.

> La gente es cobista por estupidez y, a veces, sonríen aunque en el fondo de su alma sientan una repugnancia inmensa, una repugnancia que casi no pueden contener. Por coba se puede llegar hasta el asesinato; seguramente que ha habido más de un crimen que se haya hecho por quedar bien, por dar coba a alguien. [28]

---

[26] *Ibid.*, pp. 100, 141, 179, 303.
[27] *Ibid.*, p. 154.
[28] *Ibid.*, p. 24.

Sapped of their will to be, these are the people to whom there are generic references, but whose lives are not dramatized in *La Colmena*. Their effect is that of the whole. The particular individuals who have stature in this novel may eventually be crushed and assimilated into the mass of inertia, but during their literary tenure, they are social outcasts, if not in relentless opposition, at least squirming to escape social enclosure.

Cela's attitude toward the established political rule, peripherally scornful, is basically mild. The regime is exiled into an area of insignificance. That, of course, is a greater punitive act than mere scorn. In positive terms, if *La Colmena* is an indictment at all, it is a vehement protestation against the social order of Spanish history, the caste system, the sense of honor, the concept of *el señor*, the emphasis on appearance and many other aspects of historical values which no longer fit the pattern of contemporary life. However, the element of revolt is a by-product. It is inferred by the reader as he witnesses the disproportionate lives of the people who seek to live in harmony with a past that is only weakly related to the present. The ties of history hang precariously.

In the last analysis, disapprobation is but the shadow of the lives that are illumined in this novel. Even in the creation of the most unexemplary people there is more sympathy than condemnation. Humor, grotesque though it may be, replaces traditional contempt.

        El juez interrogó a don Ibrahim.
        —Vayamos por partes. ¿La finada tenía familia?
        —Sí, señor juez, un hijo.
        —¿Dónde está?
        —¡Uf, cualquiera lo sabe, señor juez! Es un chico de malas costumbres.
        —¿Mujeriego?
        —Pues no, señor juez, mujeriego no.
        —¿Quizás jugador?
        —Pues no; que yo sepa, no.
        El juez miró para don Ibrahim.
        —¿Bebedor?
        —No, no tampoco bebedor.
        El juez ensayó una sonrisita un poco molesta.
        —Oiga usted, ¿a qué llama usted malas costumbres? ¿A coleccionar sellos?
        Don Ibrahim se picó.

>   —No, señor, yo llamo malas costumbres a muchas cosas; por ejemplo, a ser marica.
>   —¡Ah, vamos! El hijo de la finada es marica.
>   —Sí, señor juez, un marica como una catedral. [29]

In some cases the humor is translated in terms of horror as in the case of the son of the deceased and his male companion.

>   Oye, ¿por qué nos tendrán aquí?
>   —Pues no sé. ¿Tú no habrás abandonado a alguna virtuosa señorita después de hacerla un hijo? [30]

In other instances the comical aspect is quite traditional.

>   —Delante de Hitler me quedaría más azorada que una mona, debe ser un hombre que azore mucho; tiene una mirada como un tigre...
>   —Ése y el Papa, yo creo que son los dos que azoran más. [31]

Principally, *La Colmena* presents its characters in a plane of ambivalent irony, supported by a greater proportion of pity than horror. Discrepant situations suggest a laughter that is merciful rather than mordant. The realm of the ideal is at times related to the sphere of experience coarsely but compassionately.

>   Celestino estaba más locuaz que nunca.
>   —¡Adelante, pues, sin desfallecimientos y sin una sola claudicación!
>   —¡Adelante!
>   —Luchamos por el pan y por la libertad!
>   —¡Muy bien!
>   —¡Y nada más! ¡Que cada cual cumpla con su deber! ¡Adelante!
>   Celestino, de repente, sintió ganas de hacer una necesidad.
>   —¡Un momento! [32]

---

[29] *Ibid.*, p. 132.
[30] *Ibid.*, p. 151.
[31] *Ibid.*, pp. 70-71.
[32] *Ibid.*, pp. 238-239.

Celestino's situation seems ridiculously disparate. His commonplace experience does not logically attack the virtue of his ideological position, instead it gives it an ambiguous perspective. His ideology is comically profaned, but Celestino is no less a sympathetic character than he was before. The seriousness of his dreams is ludicrously destroyed by crude reality, but his propensity for dreaming absurdities is not impaired.

In gravity as in comedy, benign irony rather than virulence sets the mood of defiance in *La Colmena*. Solemnity, like hilarity, seldom has only one plane of vision. The author is able to laugh —even if it is with tears— at the inconsistencies of the Spanish people, even at their cruelty. The equivocal sense of morality is not censured; it is ridiculed. Doña Asunción who is intolerant of Elvirita's profession, even though it is forced upon the girl by the economy of hunger, takes great pride in the role of her own daughter, la Paquita. Doña Asunción is deliriously happy to learn of the death of the wife of la Paquita's lover, who is Professor of psychology, logic and ethics.

—La esposa de mi novio ha fallecido de unas anemias perniciosas. ¡Caray, doña Asunción, así ya se puede!
—Siga, siga.
—Y mi novio dice que ya no usemos nada y que si quedo en estado pues él se casa. ¡Pero, hija, si es usted la mujer de la suerte!
—Sí, gracias a Dios, tengo bastante suerte con esta hija.
—¿Y el novio es el catedrático?
—Sí, don José María de Samas, catedrático de Psicología, Lógica y Ética.
—¡Pues, hija, mi enhorabuena! Bien la ha colocado! [33]

Doña Asunción is a very devout woman. In addition to praying for the birth of a child she makes a vow.

—¡Ahora, si Dios quisiera que se quedase embarazada! ¡Eso sí que sería suerte! Su novio es un señor muy considerado por todo el mundo, no es ningún pelagatos, que es todo un catedrático. Yo he ofrecido ir a pie al Cerro de los Ángeles si la niña se queda en estado. [34]

---

[33] *Ibid.*, p. 140.
[34] *Ibid.*, p. 273.

There are countless references to the harsh structure of Spanish social order, but in most cases the persecutors appear more ridiculous than their victims, and possibly more pitiable. We feel sorry for the washerwomen of the brothels. They have descended to their lowly station after being cast from one house of prostitution to another. They now lack professional status and can afford the luxury of virtue in their physical degradation. Some of these women, like Dorita, were originally forced into nefariousness by seduction. In Dorita's particular case the culprit was a seminarist who was to attain the high office of canon of the cathedral of León. His name, Cojoncio Alba, destroys his literary personality more effectively than could diatribes or retribution. Within the foundation of social respectability, the canon cannot escape mockery, the cruel fate imposed on him as the result of a bet by his sardonic father.

Resounding laughter, often savage in nature, is heard in the abyss of depravity as well as the heights of solemnity. Conversely, there is lachrymosity in much of the comedy of *La Colmena*. The effect suggests horror. There is a feeling of guilt, self-hatred, on the part of the civilized reader who has learned to distinguish right from wrong. Against his strong moral education, he finds himself «enjoying» morbid humor and burlesque tragedy, as he experiences the drastic lives of the characters of this novel. There is a sense of shame in laughing and crying at what is morally speaking an inopportune time. Yet, there is an inevitable disproportionate alliance of laughter and tears in the reading of this novel. *La Colmena* is basically a grotesque human comedy, which dramatically reflects the malformation of its time, a disfigurement of history.

In perpetuating the scars of the Spanish Civil War, Cela captures in literature the inner life of a period which flounders in irresolute confusion. Its membranes of tradition virtually shattered by the war, the era seems but a fetus in the history of Spain, an undeveloped portion of time which lacks definite form. Only the dormant consciousness of a past and the vague dream of a future prevent its becoming a vacuum. With all its shame and sorrow the epoch survives as a literary object because it is depicted through the creation of characters who are intensely alive. The reality of the misshapen form of life in the early nineteen forties is contained in the characterization of the people. The sympathy which propels the author in forging human existence infiltrates his recreation of the habitat. His discontent with circumstances is tempered with understanding. Madrid of the post-Civil War remains alive because it is painted from within; it is given animation by the people who inhabit it in *La Colmena*.

In the fragmentary vision of man in the early nineteen forties Madrid is recreated only portionally. The description is predominantly introspective. There are hardly any detailed accounts of dwellings or settings in general. Only when their reality relates to people are actual novelistic places considered. In *La Colmena* Madrid is the conglomeration of buzzing lives who relentlessly traverse one another and move nowhere. It is man who gives his contour to his time and place.

At the beginning of the book there is a fierceness about the city that suggests a state of war between the author and his society. Cela seems violently preoccupied with establishing the atmosphere of aimless disproportion. The very first sentence alludes to the loss of a sense of proportion: «no perdamos la perspectiva...» [35] The mood is intensified by the sudden introduction of overwhelming bits of stories and glimpses of people. It is impossible to have a proportioned perspective of clarity. «No perdamos la perspectiva» is an ironical admonition. We already have. The first sight of Madrid is orderless. Only a mass of confusion can be distinguished.

As the book progresses the aura of chaotic existence does not diminish but the author's anger subsides. *La Colmena* begins without charity but it ends on a strong note of pity. The same forbidding Madrid which at first repels, later inspires compassion. Not just a pitiable compassion. Not a mere feeling of gladness proper of sympathizers, who consider themselves superior to the objects of their pity. But a feeling of compassion that includes admiration and even some envy. In the laments of the physical circumstances which surround the capital, there is esteem for the people who in their condemnation strive to transcend or at least struggle blindly with their hopeless existence. Cela's determination to paint the decadent Madrid of 1943 seems not to have taken into account the charm of many of his *madrileños*. They are not dehumanized while they are being crushed by famine and degradation. On the contrary, as the odds against them become unsurmountable, the trivialities of their lives augment in stature. Their fate which at first appeared inconsequential is now tragic;

---

[35] *Ibid.*, p. 15.

their petty joys attain gigantic proportions. The standard of measure becomes their unique values, not the author's, not the reader's. Twenty two *pesetas* are not translated into piddling cents, but in terms of human sacrifice. The economics of *La Colmena* is human dignity. This is the precious commodity.

Self-respect, a pedestrian possession for the satiated, but a luxury for the hungry, reappears throughout *La Colmena* in strange forms.[36] Pride is not eliminated. It may be no more than a gesture but it is profoundly felt. Petrita takes pride in her sacrifice; Martín Marco spends his fortune to avenge his humiliation in Doña Rosa's *café*. Even the sodomist, the repugnant Pepe, friend of *la fotógrafa*, challenges his detractors to a fight. The esteem of the self is often absurd, but a personal reality nevertheless. If the expression of human dignity does not reach the heights of absolute admiration it is because no such heights exist in Spain of the nineteen forties. The remarkable aspect is that hunger should not have destroyed completely the pride of man. The vision of humanity is not entirely pathetic; but only virtually so. Spain in seen in the process of being overcome but not yet in perfect subjugation. The element of protest though incongruously expressed, is dramatically alive in the evaporating stage setting of *La Colmena*.

In the fractional perspective of *La Colmena* there are novelistic personages who perpetuate through their lives the despair of a nation, the futility of an era. If their existence lacks the traditional well-defined finality of the 19th-century novelistic protagonist it is because the Spanish society of the post-Civil War, devoid of ideals, has no definite form. In their space and time, in the vacuum in which they reside, merely to want to be, encloses novelistic possibilities. In their society the act of conscious survival represents consumation. However feeble, any opposition is heroic, any illusion, a monumental dream. In the world of the «Outer Belt»[37] aimless defiance is lofty.

---

[36] «The profound bitterness of *The Hive* is centered in the loss of human dignity», as Barea states but it is not a complete loss in all cases. Often it is distorted but in anamolous form it does exist. Camilo José Cela, *The Hive*, Farrar, Straus and Young, N. Y., 1953, Introduction by Arturo Barea.

[37] The last words of the book, uttered by Martín Marco, tragically accentuate the absurdity of the environment. The persecuted victim of the police-state has a consciousness of the disproportion around him. «—¡Ja, ja! ¡Los pueblos del cinturón! ¡Qué chistoso! ¡Los pueblos del cinturón!» *Op. Cit.*, p. 351.

The three days of the year 1943 with which *La Colmena* is concerned are filled with the anxiety of a world at war and a nation, Spain, in the wake of its own suicidal struggle. In the setting of such a human abyss there no longer exist past criteria of magnanimity for chivalric acts. Survival itself is an accomplishment, cruelty an accepted instrument. Altruistic deviation, however slight, appears gigantic, for man is consumed with the self, that is, with the self of flesh and blood. The attrition of hunger accentuates physical reality. Merely to dream, to hope for the fulfillment of another existence is theatrical; actually to strive for such an achievement is heroic. The appearance of absurdity that the «hero» may assume does not detract from his stature as a protagonist. It just characterizes him as being part of an epoch in which symmetry is not possible. By the circumstances of history, man's own doings, grotesqueness is the national form of human existence in the Spain of the early nineteen forties.

Virtually detached from their heritage, at variance with themselves, faltering indeterminately, the people of *La Colmena* dramatically convey the spiritlessness of an era of disproportion. Outwardly the great war that rages between the Allies and the Axis powers is determining man's fate; inwardly, especially in Spain, man is pitted against himself in a sea of turbulent trivialities. There are no worlds to conquer amidst the trifling realities of living. Hermetically sealed by the despair of material constriction, human existence becomes obsessed with material reality. In the warped preoccupation with self-preservation, there is a tendency to surrender the awareness of being that helps to distinguish man from other animals. It is indeed amazing, a notable testimony of the author's basic faith in man, that this environment should enclose at all, possibilities for human exaltation.

The vision of the novelistic protagonists is quite naturally undeveloped in a literary world which lacks fulfillment. There is no sense of completeness in the art of Cela. It is deliberately unsatisfying. In the evolution of life in *La Colmena* we have before us «missing links» of history in a perspective that lacks totality in time and space. In the diffusion of partial experiences we can hope to capture only glimpses rather than a full view of the actors whose drama we are witnessing. Their growth or regression is swift and intense. There is a brusqueness about their appearance on the stage. Their exit is no more graceful. The reader who is accustomed to the art of the traditional novel is left wanting. Cela thus accomplishes the novelist's mission of transferal. The effect of frustrated reality is implanted upon the audience.

Encompassed in an atmosphere of disintegrating particles, the novelistic entities assert themselves not in the grandiose tradition of Don Quijote, nor in the bourgeois glory of Madame Bovary, but merely by distinguishing themselves from the droning mass of existence that envelops them. By virtue of sheer momentary resistance to commonality they are extraordinary; in their spurts of defiance they loom as august. It is a fleeting impression, but in the evanescent reality of their realm it represents fruition.[38] Eternity is evaluated in terms of the instant, for the whole need not exist. Thus, it is possible for Martín Marco, the central figure of *La Colmena*, to bring about in his tortuous way the intertwining of lives. He serves as the junction for events and in some instances he is the force that incites novelistic action as in the case of Petrita. Whereas Martín's stature as a hero might not fit the pattern of tradition, in the world that is Spain after the Civil War, he wears well the histrionic clothes of the paladin.

Among the women —and it is primarily the female sex which conserves any vestige of traditional vigor in the society of *La Colmena*—, Petrita and Victorita emerge as tragic characters of eminent magnitude. With an unpredictive agonizing resoluteness, untypical of their time and place, they affirm themselves in rebellious defiance against their destiny. Moreover, they strive to forge fate in their own image. Viewed solely from the security of the dollar economy, a most unliterary approach, their trivial conflicts may seem unworthy of human sacrifice. Translated in terms of their own circumstances their personal struggles are monumental. In their tormentive, sporadic attempts to chart the course of their lives they are majestic figures.

Until the moment of decision Petrita bears with placid dignity the impossibility of her dreams. And in her determination to render her illusions liveable, to give form to her fantasy Petrita, the maid, maintains queenly demeanor. It is she who wills her fate. In her defilement she enhances her position of defiance. Her spirit of rebel-

---

[38] My early interpretation of Cela's novels, made in the image of the past, was anachronistic. It was an error of historical perspective on my part to attempt to judge Cela's characters in the tradition of the art of Cervantes and Galdós. *Hispania*, «Spain in the Novels of Cela and Baroja,» March, 1958.

lion becomes more intense. Flauntingly she imperils the security of her betrothal as she clamors her devotion for her idol, symbolically incarnated in the person of Martín Marco. In her submission Petrita has the regal beauty of a lioness. [39]

The driving force that converts Petrita into a novelistic protagonist emanates from within her realm of personal existence. The material state of Spain may shape the form of her conversion, but it is not the determining factor in her growth as a literary character. That is to say, hunger obliges her to debase herself for the paltry sum of 22 *pesetas,* a veritable fortune for her, but it is not hunger that incites her abstract love for Martín Marco. The influence that is exerted on her transcends circumstances of environment. The ideal love which Martín Marco inspires in Petrita recalls the mythical influence of Dulcinea del Toboso on Don Quijote. And just as the unseen Lady of Toboso becomes the knight errant's reason for being, Martín Marco assumes the role of the prime mover in Petrita's existence.

The maid's plane of reality is not romantically unidimensional; she has a multilateral novelistic existence. Her moments of grandeur are dynamically intermingled with her prosaic position as a maid and as the plebeian fiancée of an ordinary simple policeman. Petrita reaches heights of human exaltation and novelistically descends to depths of coarse reality. Like thousands of other maids who steal out of their master's home to join their fiancés after work is done, Petrita makes love with the Galician policeman, Julio García Mazarro, in the wasteplot that is the rendezvous for the poor.

Although the personal predicament of Victorita is embedded in the economic plight of Spain, the shop girl herself shapes her form of confrontation with circumstances. «Victorita tenía fuerza de voluntad...» [40] In opposition to her domineering mother, she persists in maintaining her unpromising engagement to her tubercular fiancé, Paco. And from him, who constitutes the impulse for her dazzling dreams but who, himself, is submerged in apathetic decay, she receives no direction. Enmeshed in ubiquitious despair, Victorita almost succumbs to the indigenous deliverances of her society. «Desde irse monja hasta hacer la carrera.» [41] Beset with the hostility and cruel

---

[39] See note 14.
[40] *Ibid.,* p. 219.
[41] *Ibid.,* p. 225.

languor of the world around her, in the turmoil of her solipsistic existence, the eighteen-year old girl musters her will and in agonizing tremor affirms herself as a novelistic character.

In her fall as in her rise, Victorita maintains her dignity. Assailed with doubts about her decision, she retains a consciousness of her migratory planes of reality. Unlike a romantic martyr of nineteenth century literature, Victorita lives the uncertainty of her venture. While wishing to believe herself indomitable in her resoluteness to create a new life for herself and Paco, her trembling body betrays her fears. In striving to attain an abstract ideal of economic security she is intransigent; in the dramatic moment of rendering her dream into concrete reality she is possessed with fearful vacilation. Ultimately she surrenders to the allurement of her dream, but not without incessant struggle. The conflict continues to rage within her when she reaches a verdict and when the moment of imposing sentence upon herself arrives.

The most amazing aspect of Cela's literary achievement, his stroke of genius, is his ability to capture human tragedy and comedy in a desultory style, that is the trademark of *La Colmena*. Within a few photographic pages, their negative form not fully developed, the author succeeds in creating novelistic characters whose livingness gives reality to the portrayal of an era of Hispanic existence. It is by means of creating strikingly real people that the author makes the era come alive. Through the characters a bond of sympathy is established with Madrid in the year 1943.

The microscopic three days of *La Colmena* reveal the core of a singular epoch which is virtually detached from its past. In this speck of time the author dramatizes his own experience of Spain's total historical existence. Out of Cela's vision of Spain, embedded in the disproportion of the present with the past, possibly in terms of personal disillusionment, comes forth the perspective of unsymmetrical fragmentation that constitutes the symphonic theme of the novel. Only the rise of novelistic characters and situations transcends the recurrent melody of dissonance. Cela's vision of Spain constitutes the abstractness of *La Colmena*; his novelistic achievement gives concrete meaning to his artistically distorted perspective. The personal conflicts of Petrita and Victorita, the aimless wanderings of Martín Marco incarnate in a uniquely disjunctive manner the single organic reality of a given time and space.

Although peripherally the recreation of three days of life in Madrid suggests a view of undistinguishable humanity groping for survival, actually there is revealed in this agglomeration of fractional existence the expression of rebellious lives who tower above the natural circumstances of their experiences. Perhaps in a subliminal manner, these characters constitute Cela's «strident voice in the desert».[42] Theirs are the voices that resound perturbably long after the spectacle of arid land evaporates into obliviousness. And the situations that are salvaged from imminent dissolution in *La Colmena* are given perdurable life by the sympathetic creatures who struggle to achieve personal form in opposition to the relentless mass of indistinction that threatens to overwhelm them.

In addition to Petrita, Victorita, and Martín Marco, a gallery of sympathetic characters in their embryonic formation, rise from the depths of mass life to imprint fractions of their personalities in the morass into which they are sinking. One can hardly forget the man who commits suicide because his mouth smells of onions. Had the victim's wife been able to speak, the author tells us, when she was asked what happened, she would have said: «—Nada, que olía un poco a cebolla.»[43] Nor can one erase from his memory the awkward situation of the man who died in a «third class brothel». His friends wishing to conceal the grotesqueness of his death dress him and bring him home to his wife. Although the suspenders are left behind, doña Juana, the wife of the deceased, in her conjugal devotion, overlooks the detail. She has no doubt of her late husband's ultimate destination. «¡Lo único que me reconforta es pensar que se ha ido derechito al cielo...»[44] Nor does one find it simple not to recall how Elvirita, the prostitute, puts herself to sleep with prayers over an empty stomach. Then, she is too proud to admit to the gluttonous doña Rosa that unlike the wealthy *café* owner, she need not worry lest overeating interfere with her sleep. In all cases, these and hundreds of others, the quest for dignity, however incongruous the results, gives the episodes a sense of respectability. In their strange ways, many are the people who, if unable to combat, attempt to squirm out of their mire with some degree of dignity.

---

[42] See note 6.
[43] *Ibid.*, p. 290.
[44] *Ibid.*, p. 272.

The horror of human disintegration enclosed within the physical reality of hunger constitutes the outer fabric of *La Colmena*, its façade. Beyond this layer of appearance lies the inner structure of the novel, its foundation. Within the aura of constrictive decay that pervades the novel, life grows and expands. Reminiscent of the Hell of Dante, amidst abjection, the beauty of living is exalted. Already manifest in Cela's earlier novels, the joy for life blooms with fulminating vigor in *La Colmena*. Contained in a receptacle of despair, doomed to evaporation, human existence affirms itself as a sublime experience in its fragmentary moments of vitality.

The first words of *La Colmena* «no perdamos la perspectiva» might serve as an admonition for the discriminating reader. To be submerged in the panorama of annihilation is to lose our sense of proportion. It is not hunger that sustains the structure of this book. As in some fantastic architecture, the pillars of this book are the living novelistic people who are cemented unto one another with sympathy.

VI. MRS. CALDWELL HABLA CON SU HIJO

Cela's fifth novel, *Mrs. Caldwell habla con su hijo* (1953), constitutes the most prominent paradigm of his bizarre art. The charm of the book rests largely on its enigmatic aspect. *Mrs. Caldwell habla con su hijo* is provocatively mystifying. Its seemingly simple structure encompasses undefinable images which defy enclosure.[1] In the last analysis, the reality of the book will reflect the readers' experiences. This novel, more than any other of Cela, demands participation on the part of the audience. Completeness would destroy it. Thus, the novel will take the form of the personal moment. It may be an allegory; it may be a satire; it may be the profound confession of guilt of an errant mother; it may be sheer poetry, and possibly sheer madness. At times it is all of these things and more, and then there are moments when it seems to be an ineffable experience —like so many of our world— which we will never fully comprehend.

In the guise of a dialogue, although in fact only one person is speaking, *Mrs. Caldwell habla con su hijo* presents a series of soliloquies which purportedly are written in the form of letters. The writings of the mother are said to have been recovered in an insane asylum where she died as a patient. At the time of compostion, the son was already dead. So we have as the grotesque format of the book letters of an insane mother to her dead son. The fact that Mrs. Caldwell, an Englishwoman, inexplicably writes in excellent Spanish adds a further note of incongruity.

---

[1] «*Mrs. Caldwell* es un libro que no me acabo de explicar.» Juan Luis Alborg, *Hora Actual de la Novela Española*, Madrid, Taurus, 1958, p. 95. In stating that he was unable to explain *Mrs. Caldwell habla con su hijo* to himself, Señor Alborg was beginning to understand it.

Mrs. Caldwell habla con su hijo could be interpreted as an allegory in which Spain, with the grief of a mother who has lost her only son, speaks to the Spaniards who have died in the Civil War. Lunacy paves the way for confession. In her madness, Mrs. Caldwell can afford the luxury of the naked truth. [2] The English name, perhaps a personal allusion, [3] would, then, represent a nationality other than that which it pretends to be. A perspective of symbolism, however valid, might suggest ramifications and open the way to endless schematic evaluations. Especially in the intricate creative process of Cela's novels, each interpretation might contain an element of intuitive truth.

As a satire, the novel could be viewed as the cruel reflection of a mother's selfish love for her son. There are instances when Mrs. Caldwell's expression of affection evokes Freudian symbols. Her feelings are more of a spouse than of a mother. And in her avowed consideration of her son's welfare, she may appear totally submerged in supreme ego-centricity. It would, then, not be a lamentation of her son's fate, but rather an utterance of self-pity. The more she pretends to be engulfed in the life of her son, the more she tells us of her own experiences. In her avowed intent to make Eliacim the protagonist, she concentrates the narration on herself. It is she who emerges as the principal figure. Her son is an abstraction. Perhaps *Mrs. Caldwell habla con su hijo* is a satire on what we believe to be the loftiest of human feelings, maternal love. If this be the case, Mrs. Caldwell might well be the incarnation of Pascual Duarte's mother. Insanity may be a more cruel fate than death.

As an intimate account of a mother's confession to her son who can no longer hear, the novel is a sublimely pathetic expression of a mind full of guilt, unable to live with itself. In revealing her innermost secrets, she discloses the sins of her life in fact and in fancy. Guilty of adultery, Mrs. Caldwell relates to her son the identity of his real father. In the realm of imagination, she displays her passionate incestuous love for Eliacim, her beloved son. Divested of the sense of social shame proper of a sane mind, in her uninhibited state

---

[2] The escape into madness for the revelation of truth is, of course, in the Cervantian tradition. Unamuno too has preached that we need to divest ourselves of reason in order to attain truth.

[3] Cela's mother was English. As a child, the author understood the English language; now, as a mature person, he gives the impression of being frightened by the Anglo-Saxon sounds.

Mrs. Caldwell is capable of enduring dissective introspection. Her profound feeling of culpability appears to be based not on the course of her erratic life but rather on her failure to have communicated more intimately with her son while he was alive. Her frustration is that which the living experience for the dead. Her desire is to fill the absolute vacuum which exists between life and death.

Considered as pure lyricism, the words of Mrs. Caldwell abound with a poetic reality which transcends the grasp of reason. Virtually everything in the novel is expressed in terms of imagery. The book is more suggestive than expository. There is more expression than communication. The concepts of life and death are embodied in the personal intangible experiences of the mad mother. Having ascended from the plane of reason to one of feeling, Mrs. Caldwell attains a state of sublimity. Logic will not discern the lofty state of the Englishwoman; reason will not decipher its mysteries.

An objective scientific approach to literature might convince us that the book is sheer madness. That too would be true. Are the words not that of a proven lunatic? If madness can be ascertained by virtue of social reason, Mrs. Caldwell is mad. And no question is raised in the novel as to the possibility that the protagonist may be well of mind. No attempt is made to suggest that the suffering mother has possession of her faculties. Indeed, she is mad and her words are madness. But her illness is contagious.

Mrs. Caldwell habla con su hijo represents a fascinating novelistic technique which defies classification. In a sense it exceeds Cela's own incongruous pattern of writing. That is to say, it gives his writings an air of fantasy. The first four novels are enclosed in an atmosphere of harsh physical reality; the fifth one has as its setting the hallucinatory recollection of a demented mind. Yet, in its turbulent diffusion of personal experiences the accounts of Mrs. Caldwell bring us into a world of undefinable inner reality which possibly has more palpability than empirical sensations.

In its format, *Mrs. Caldwell habla con su hijo* constitutes a collection of outwardly unrelated essays which are capricious in nature. Held togeher by the exotic personality of the main character, the essays are in themselves lyrical entities of the intellect. Each one expresses an abstract thought or recalls a personal event. By means of these *morceaux* Mrs. Caldwell unfolds as a character who evokes a strange inexplicable attraction. Whether or not one can logically share Mrs. Caldwell's feelings, he is impressed by her profound sensitivity to all aspects of life, the gigantic and the trivial. Interwoven in a monstruous arabesque pattern, without a sense of discrimination for the large and for the small, the experience of life is captured with a disproportionate relentless fervor that perhaps can exist only in madness. Unrestrained by a sense of equilibrium, Mrs. Caldwell's feeling for life knows no bounds.

With intensity, the mind of Mrs. Caldwell flows in a stream of consciousness. She brings together humor and pathos, irony and satire, clarity and disparity. At times she is frighteningly logical. In some instances she displays a poetic vision; in other cases, she borders on crudity. Sensitive to delicacy, she is also cruel. The totality of her life is humanly self-contradictory, but she lives her paradoxes as inherent and irreducible traits of her personality. There is something about her character that appeals to man's super-logic. Perhaps Mrs. Caldwell candorously reveals an essential disorder which civilized man through the chains of science or religion will not rationally accept. In *Mrs. Caldwell habla con su hijo*, without order there is beauty, without order there is life.

In the preceding novel of Cela, *La Colmena*, the reality of living was captured through the experiences of hundreds of characters. In *Mrs. Caldwell habla con su hijo* the literary experience of life is created through the existence of one principal personage. Naturally, in Mrs. Caldwell's retrospective analysis there are a host of characters, but essentially they remain undefined. They are essentially impressionistic undeveloped entities. They do not necessarily represent the incentive or literary pretext for Mrs. Caldwell's expression. Being mad, Mrs. Caldwell need not have any superimposed motivation to guide her. She speaks to her son because her own sense of living begins with motherhood. The multiplication of the self gives Mrs. Caldwell her sense of being. Eliacim is the mirror of her life.

The wandering mind of Mrs. Caldwell knows no limits in its perspective of the animate world. As in all other books of Cela, the preoccupation is with the living of life. In recalling the existence of her dead son, Mrs. Caldwell, from the very beginning concentrates on the account of his life as it relates to her own. Even when she refers to his last moments on earth, she emphasizes her son's concern over his impending burial. As death approaches, Eliacim [4] reveres life. He is troubled by the possibility that the funeral procession, his grand departure, may not have the effect of proper luxury.

> Cuando falleció, le hicimos un entierro de segunda clase porque no estábamos en situación demasiado holgada. Él, el pobre, bien lo sintió. Poco antes de morir, no hacía más que preguntarme ¿tú no crees que pidiéndole algo de dinero al señor del segundo, que siempre estuvo tan propicio, podríamos juntar para un entierro de primera? [5]

As the book is about to end, Mrs. Caldwell sees herself in Hell, dying in flames, but there are no regrets for life. The fire burns in the living and Mrs. Caldwell faces her inquisition almost with delight, certainly without fear.

> No me asustó nada, amor mío, ver mi habitación llena de fuego, ver mi habitación ardiendo, ver mi habitación rebosante de cautelosas llamas que me abrasaban la carne...
> Pero aunque sé que el fuego de mi habitación es devastador y maldito, amor mío, y de la misma substancia que el fuego del infierno, me siento muy dichosa de saberte testigo de él, excepcional y apasionado testigo de él. [6]

All that is living is joyful to Mrs. Caldwell. In her stage role, she wears the mask of Oscar Wilde's ironical aphorism that every experience is a good one. The cursed air that is Spain. The execrable breath of life. The crudest atmosphere of her habitat. All that is life becomes part of Mrs. Caldwell's living experience.

> Allá donde se aman los gatos más escuálidos y sarnosos, donde se asfixian los músicos que se volvieron tísicos de tocar la corneta, donde se pudren las cabezas de los pescados, donde orina el vendedor ambulante, donde da de mamar a sus hijos la sonrosada rata del cólera, donde se citan los más tímidos

---

[4] Professor R. S. Willis of Princeton University has raised the question of a possible anagram in the name *Eliacim*. In a letter to me, Professor Willis wonders whether the name could mean *Eliakim* (Hebrew: «God establishes»). He further adds «...but where does that take us?» It certainly adds another dimension to the interpretation of the book.

[5] *Mrs. Caldwell habla con su hijo*, p. 23.

[6] *Ibid.*, p. 221.

ladrones, donde se siente el frío más abyecto, donde nadie se acuerda de sonreír, vive ese aire maldito que duerme entre las casas...

Todo es cuestión, hijo mío, de acostumbrarse a respirar ese aire maldito que duerme entre las casas.

Hay días en los que me sería imposible olvidarme de él, imposible vivir sin él. [7]

Mrs. Caldwell's logic has a piercing quality of incompleteness. Reason raises more questions than it solves. Her views on work and idleness are sensible within the pattern of Biblical credulity. But more than rational, they are expressive of a way of life which may be at the same time exquisite and damnable. In seriousness or in comedy, her observations are penetrating; there is a disturbing truth about them.

¿Es Pecado el Trabajo?...

El hombre no fue creado para trabajar sino para holgar y no comer del árbol prohibido. Sólo cuando pecó y fue expulsado del Paraíso, se encontró con que tenía que ganarse el pan con el sudor de su frente.

No amemos las maldiciones de Jehová. No caigamos en la blasfemia.

El Ocio...

Es provechoso el ocio, hijo mío; el ocio es un amable regalo de los dioses, una benévola bendición de los dioses. Yo pienso, Eliacim, que si se pudiese almacenar el ocio, si se pudiese manufacturar y comerciar con él como sucede con otros productos, se llegaría a prestar un gran servicio a los hombres. [8]

Underneath the reasoning which would extol the Hispanic mode of being is a note of plaintive expression. Logically the contention is tenable, and yet it is unsatisfying. In some instances Mrs. Caldwell's derangement consists in the super-abundance of ratiocination.

Mrs. Caldwell's disorderly mind represents a fertile field for the cultivation of logical and illogical expressions. Here prose merges

---

[7] *Ibid.*, pp. 144-45.
[8] *Ibid.*, pp. 49 and 141.

with poetry. And often what may seem like the repetitious rantings of a lunatic acquires poetic stature.

El Iceberg

>Hijo mío, querido:
>Navegando sin brújula, el iceberg, contigo encima, vuela a una velocidad increíble.
>El iceberg, contigo encima, vuela a una velocidad increíble, navegando sin brújula.
>Contigo encima, el iceberg, navegando sin brújula, vuela a una velocidad increíble.
>Vuela a una velocidad increíble, contigo encima, el iceberg navegando sin brújula. [9]

The nearly fifty lines of her recurrent thought are tauto-phonically converted into a musical refrain. The superfluous truth of logic becomes a hymn to her dead son.

Beside the poetic utterances are found voices of crudity and cruel irony. The aimless ramblings of Mrs. Caldwell's cries follow an irregular pattern of behavior. Her aberrations exalt and degrade.

>El joven oficial de caballería cuidaba, estallante de mimo, a su madre vieja y paralítica, una pobre señora que se hacía sus necesidades por encima...
>Dorothy... ha muerto en el hospital. (No me gustó verla envuelta en aquella sábana que nada la favorecía... [10]

Deliberately without any traditional sense of proportion, the structure of the novel is explosive. The detonative qualities of the book erupt fiercely, without warning. The contemplative moments of passivity are also strikingly unexpected so as to be felt with an intensity that anticipates volcanic intrusion. There is no prescribed order in the fire that rages within the disorderly mind of the heroine, Mrs. Caldwell.

Mrs. Caldwell habla con su hijo is a novel of disorder. In a state of vital derangement, in anticipation of her own annihilation, the novelistic protagonist recalls her living past, that is to say, the past as

---

[9] *Ibid.*, p. 180.
[10] *Ibid.*, pp. 115 and 150.

it is experienced in the present. Unlike the account of Pascual Duarte, there is no sense of topical chronology in the evocations of Mrs. Caldwell. In *La Familia de Pascual Duarte* the reader wonders about the event that determined the hero's fate. There is no such curiousity about Mrs. Caldwell, whose madness is an integral part of her being. Her fate rests not on occurences but rather on her own living experience of the world in which she is born. We accept Mrs. Caldwell as being congenitally mad in the novelistic sense, as though madness were as natural a characteristic as a physical trait. Accordingly, her chameleonic perspective of life is understandably nomadic; its one fixed feature is its constant disorder.

Perhaps the most disturbing aspect of this novel is that literary reality should exist in an atmosphere of chaos. Characters are created as believable entities in the anomalous vision of Mrs. Caldwell. However hallucinatory they may be, the heroine's remembrance of things past establishes a core of identity with the reader's own vage —and often imaginary— recollection of bygone experiences. Moreover, Mrs. Caldwell's complex personality attains an intense sense of concreteness as her impressionistic experiences are revealed. Within the unsymmetrical perspective of life that is created, the Englishwoman fulfills the role of a tragic figure. She has defied destiny and she has fallen from grace. Conscious of the fire that rages within her, Mrs. Caldwell is prepared for her imminent destruction. Only in inevitable nihilism is there a sense of solidarity, and thus Mrs. Caldwell, awaiting obliteration, puts her house in order.[11] If life was turbulent and indefinable, death is serene and orderly.

The reading of *Mrs. Caldwell habla con su hijo* is a poetic experience. Reason alone will not capture the essence of the work. The lyrical poetry of human turmoil, the inexplicable confusion of man, represents a challenge to the reader's intellect, a delight to his artistic senses. There is in the work a clamor for the joy of living which suggests a type of existential hedonism, an adoration of agonizing life.

---

[11] «No puedo con el agua que cae del techo, amor mío, que mana de las paredes, que brota del suelo, que fluye de los muebles, y de las ropas de la cama, y de los objetos que tengo colocados sobre el tocador, incluso con un cierto buen orden.» *Ibid.,* p. 222.

VII. LA CATIRA

La Catira, Cela's last work to be denominated «a novel» by the publishers, is characterized by romantic savagery. Published in 1954, *La Catira* exotically, and perhaps superficially so, dedicates itself to the portrayal of primitive life in the wilds of Venezuela. In its attempt to intone epic qualities, the novel at its best succeeds in becoming a fantasy, at its worst, a sort of unwilling *esperpento*. Even its earthly poetic passages do not remove from the work an aura of super-imposed romanticism. There is an evident schism between the novelist and his topic; Cela writes as a stranger. His efforts to capture the meaning of his setting are conscientious and deliberate, but there is a lack of personal feeling which cannot be experienced by means of determination alone. There is more meaning to his desire to escape the problem of Spain than to his rational endeavor to write of a land which is alien to him.

There are in *La Catira* the external ingredients that identify the art of Cela. The work is in itself an expression of a disparate agony of life. The world of *La Catira* rests on the relentless self-destruction of nature and man. But here the image of reality does not survive Without the forging of concrete characters who impress us as being believable men of flesh and blood, the novel is an abstraction. The protagonists of *La Catira* do not give us the literary illusion of truth. As a result, we are confronted with the creation of a poetic skeleton, as it were, a symphony with the proper notes but without the fulfillment of music.

The title of the novel, which designates the principal character, Pipía Sánchez, «la hembra fuerte de la Pachequera», is not nearly so revealing as the name of the would-be series that the author gives to this work, *Historias de Venezuela*. It seems obvious that Cela's intent was not merely to write a novel in which Venezuela was the locale, but rather to compose a novel *of* Venezuela, one in which the scene would emerge as the living protagonist. Cela immortalized Madrid of the early forties in *La Colmena;* in *La Catira* he consciously sought to repeat the intuitive process with a South American country to which he came as a visitor. As a literary experiment, the work is fascinating. *La Catira* adds a new dimension to Cela's art. Here we have a perspective of the novelist who confronts himself with the problems of creating a novel almost completely objectively. A significant contribution of *La Catira* is to give us an insight of the artist at work, fleeing from the reality of his experience into a world not wholly his own.

Cela appears to be seduced by the linguistic phenomena of Venezuela. There is evidence of zealous wonderment in the compilation of the «vocabulario de venezonalismos», an integral appendix to *La Catira*. The dictionary study of the shades and meaning of words and phrases, at times peculiar to Venezuela, often characteristic of greater areas of Spanish-America, gives testimony to the novelist's bewitchment with the language of his characters. In defining «venezonalismos» Cela reveals his own discoveries, the newness of his stylistic devices. In brief, Cela is justifying the language to himself as well as to the readers; more to himself if his readers are to include natives of Venezuela.

More than any other of his novels, *La Catira* presents a portrait of Cela forging a novel. In this work the author is one of his own characters. And the book is at its best precisely when he is describing himself or other Spaniards.

> En una de sus visitas a Caracas, a don Filiberto le presentaron a un gallego medio vagabundo, que se llamaba Evaristo. Evaristo, antes, cuando era persona de provecho, se llamaba Camilo...
>
> ... —¿Y usted dice que le es de Padrón?
> —Sí, señor, yo le vengo a ser de Iria. [1]

---

[1] Camilo José Cela, *La Catira*, Barcelona, Editorial Noguer, S. A., 1955, pp. 18 and 120.

Cela cannot escape Spain and his own circumstances. In writing of Venezuela he may be poetic; in his treatment of Spain he is novelistic. The theme of his personal experiences recurs. The Spaniard is recreated with benign irony; the Spanish regime is the object of ridicule.

> Evaristo, como era español, tenía cierta tendencia a echar discursos. Evaristo, de joven, hubiera querido ser gobernador civil, pero no lo hicieron porque tenía un primo que no iba a misa más que el día del Apóstol. [2]

Ever present in *La Catira*, be it in its literary content or in its appendix, is the personality of Cela, the Spaniard relating himself to his own intimate environment of language and life.

In the creation of Venezuelan characters and provincial language there is an emptiness of content. Rationally, one could not argue with the faithful reproduction of barbarisms. Unquestionably, the people in the novel may have their imaginative counterparts in the realm of experience. Yet, there is an undefinable lack of truth in their roles as characters. Perhaps the novel is too intensely real to have the air of drama. Perhaps the effort to recreate Venezuelan life is more scholarly than artistic. In any case, the effect is not that of a work of art which stands apart as a finished entity. The image that we have of *La Catira* is that of a sculptor struggling to give life to an unfinished statue.

The elements of horror and pity that characterize *La Catira* are basically romantic. For the most part they are unrelated, and seldom are they contained in each other as is the case with Cela's other novels. In fact, in this work the characters seem to be created for the effect of emotions. They do not evolve within a milieu of barbarity; on the contrary, their actions are designed so as to give meaning to the world they inhabit. The characters are the theatrical props; the intent of the artist is to make the land the protagonist.

In the horror of sodomy and rape, in the ferocity of human malevolence, it is the poetic language of Cela that gives meaning to savage destruction.

---

[2] *Ibid.*, p. 19.

> El indio Consolación murió con los ojos abiertos y la boca cerrada. El indio Consolación murió sin ver y sin hablar. También murió sin explicarse nada, el indio Consolación.[3]

There is in this novel horror in love and horror in hate. «La india María» with profound affection buries her husband, who died in his attempt to defend her honor, while she prepares with glee a feast for the vultures with the body of her wrongdoer, Trinidad Pamplona.

> La india María enterró al indio Consolación. La india María le tapó los ojos al indio Consolación con un pañuelo, para que no se le llenasen de tierra...
>
> La india María arrastró de un pie al cadáver del guate Trinidad Pamplona. La india María lo dejó en medio del campo, en un calvero del yerbazal, con la cara levantada para que los zamuros le vaciasen los ojos. Y le mondasen las carnes hasta dejarlo en la pura güesamenta.[4]

The episode ends on a note of sentimentality, quoting a proverb that suggests that every action has its reason.

> La india María—un hijo a la espalda y otro a cada mano—se alejó de La Boba dejando atrás, y ya perdido, el tiempo en el que fue feliz, con el indio Consolación al lado, con el indio Consolación encima. La india María, antes de irse, pegó candela al ranchito, se sentó a verlo arder y no se fue hasta que se llevó el viento el último humo de la fogarera.
>
> Después, empezó a andar. El plateado alcaraván, que la vio venir, alzó el vuelo alborotando el llano con su temor. Por el Guárico, por el Apure, por Barinas, los peones lo saben: alcaraván que se espanta, gente que pasa a zorro que lo levanta.[5]

Encompassed in retributory fatalism the novel continues on its march of inevitable doom, sometimes clearly defined, in other instances merely implied. From the very beginning there is the omen of cruel disfiguration.

---

[3] *Ibid.*, p. 97.
[4] *Ibid.*, pp. 102-103.
[5] *Ibid.*, p. 103.

> Don Filiberto Marqués ni aún miró para Clorindo López. Clorindo López, la verdad por delante, tampoco tenía mucho que mirar. Tuerto y con dos dedos de menos, su pinta recordaba la del araguato. Hace ya muchos años, de niños, don Filiberto Marqués le atapuzó una pedrada a Clorindo López y le saltó un ojo. En el juraco, Clorindo López llevaba una vendita negra, tiñosa y confitera, banquete y hartazón de jejenes. Los dedos se los había comido, aún mozo, una buba maligna. [6]

Contained in the torment of savage existence, the world of *La Catira* gives form to destruction. In this novel, life is done and undone in a pre-determined pattern of consonance. Here nihilism blossoms as an expected phenomenon. Creation leads to destruction. And though the work ends on a note of future human propogation, we know that its ultimate purpose—that of dying— is inherent in birth. To engender is to destroy.

In attempting to give form to annihilation Cela departs from the art that distinguishes his previous novels. In a sense, *La Catira*, with its symmetrical imagery, neatly encased in expressions of sentimentality, completes a cycle of artistic irregularity. With the writing of *La Catira* Cela makes amends with the literary past and returns to the tradition of the romantic novel. Whether this signals his end as a novelist or merely indicates his versatility, time—and he—will tell.

Within the enclosure of *sensiblerie* there are sparks of novelistic irony that seem to suggest that Cela has not completely surrendered to the eulogy of a primitive habitat. If Cela's imagery gives poetic meaning to *La Catira*, it is his sense of wry humor that elevates the work to the sphere of the novel. Irony punctures the balloon of fantasy and brings myth to the realm of human experience.

> Evaristo empezó a temblar. Evaristo no temía a los hombres pero sentía pánico cuando la tara negra—¡sampablo, la tara negra!—le empujaba al brumoso mundo de las ánimas y los aparecidos...
>
> Evaristo, por lo bajo, estaba rezando el señormíojesucristo a toda velocidad. Cada cual se defiende del miedo como puede. [7]

---

[6] *Ibid.*, p. 13.
[7] *Ibid.*, p. 199.

The name of «Jesusito Moisés», which identifies one of the peons, is repeated numerous times until the incongruity becomes grotesque. In part, because of his name, much is expected of the peon whose actions belie the high ideals superimposed on him.

> Este pión Jesusito Moisés es tercio e confianza, comae; este pión Jesusito Moisés es un Juan Mimba e mucha responsabilidá, ¿sabe?
> El peón Jesusito Moisés, por lo bajo, murmuró algo así como:
> —¡Su madre, qué toñeco el muchacho!
> Pero por fuera se calló y se fue en busca de la negra Cándida José, para que le diese una copa de aguardiente a cambio de dejarse poner mercuricromo. [8]

Jesusito Moisés encloses within his cosmic identification possibilities of all kinds. His personality is as elastic as that of the *pícaro*.

> Jesusito Moisés era tercio entrón y sonriente, que lo mismo servía para un roto que para un descosido. [9]

Jesusito Moisés, who bears the outward mark of exalted idealism, is a most practical man.

The glimmers of novelistic irony in *La Catira* spare no one, not even the author himself. «Esto de la poesía es un entretenimiento muy para cojos; además, y a pesar de lo que digan, no hace daño a nadie.» [10] In addition to having the perspective of a novelist who is novelizing, we have the view of Cela watching himself create. These departures from the generally romantic theme of *La Catira* give meaning to the inner structure of Cela's art which is dynamically in a state of search. The quest for fulfillment is the most interesting part of the experiment. The ultimate effect of artistic harmony or dissonance is basically anti-climactic. Considered as effect, *La Catira* is disappointing; as a living experiment, it is fascinating. That is to say, the value of the novel rests on the experience that we have of the author struggling to achieve his purpose rather than on the work itself.

---

[8] *Ibid.*, p. 213.
[9] *Ibid.*, p. 227.
[10] *Ibid.*, p. 227.

In brief, the success or failure to create a Venezuelan epic is subordinate to the drama of Cela's endeavor. In the last analysis, the author is his own protagonist in *La Catira*.

Cela's appearance as a character in the novel gives *La Catira* the lyrical quality of a book of travel in which the personal perspective of the author colors the view of the land. In many aspects *La Catira* resembles the peregrinatory accounts of the author more than his other works which are denominated *novels*. In the literary exploration of the wilds of Venezuela, Cela is fundamentally following the pattern of his travel books on Spain. Naturally, his experience of the Spanish provinces needs no intermediaries; in *La Catira* the characters bind the author to his locale. They are the catalytic agents. Viewed as an account of the author's travels in a strange land, *La Catira* acquires another dimension. The work then becomes the literary experience of a voyageur in search of spiritual refuge. In this case, of one who must endeavor to escape the agony of Spain.

That he does not succeed in withdrawing from his environment is evident in his creation of Spanish characters and his recurrent allusions to his native country—to which the author returns after his brief sojourn in Venezuela.

Beset by the circumstances that forbade the publication of *La Familia de Pascual Duarte* and *La Colmena* in Spain, overcome by the apathy of his countrymen, especially by their trivial escapes from reality, Cela finds himself as a little island in the sea. Cela withdraws in anger and resentment. Spain is to be punished by his departure. He will now write of another theme, one more beautiful—if less real to him. This might be the interpretation of Cela's dual role as author and character of *La Catira*. Irreducibly integrated in this double image of himself, Cela takes revenge on Spain and his unknowing public. The chasm that existed between the author and his readers had been dramatized in form of letters in *Mrs. Caldwell habla con su hijo*. In his sixth novel, Cela dramatizes his withdrawal from the Spanish scene. In effect, he flees from his battle ground. Since 1954 Cela's novelistic «voice in the desert» has been still.

VIII. CELA'S WANDERLUST

Cela's novels do not fulfill the author's search for the meaning of Spanish life. The novels are too far removed from the personal existence of the novelist. Cela, who views his own life novelistically, [1] cannot be satisfied with being a mere creator; he must also be the leading character in his own literary intrigues. [2] In his books of travels, Cela finds self-expression. Here he appears with the total force of his literary-personal self. Here he can blend physical and imaginative realities freely, almost whimsically. He need not be inhibited even by a sense of respect for his own themes or characters. In the complex vastness of Spain just about every experience is possible.

The books of travels are quasi-novels. There are no significant characters who stand apart from the literary personality of the author. Cela dominates the scene. With the possible exception of the land, which is in a sense the other main character, the literary persons and situations do not challenge Cela's role of preeminence. However novelistic the momentary experiences may be, we cannot forget that Camilo José Cela is a man of flesh and blood. Even in the moments of intense creative irony, when the realm of physical reality joins the plane of myth, we have before us the vision of Cela, the puppeteer, pulling the strings of his puppets, including himself.

---

[1] In talking about himself Cela is a sincere actor who intermingles fact and fancy. In his mind literature and life are so blended that he has trouble distinguishing one from the other.

[2] In an excellent article entitled «Una tierra, un escritor, un libro, una edición», the Spanish poet Luis Felipe Vivanco has explored Cela's compulsion to travel. «Cuadernos Hispanoamericanos», números 128-129.

Cela's accounts of his travels in Spain are unique literary creations. They are more than «travel books». They constitute an integral part of his novelistic art. Although they are at times objectively informative, they are fundamentally lyrical novels in which the author brings together fact and fantasy. Through the literary personality of the author the towns and people of Spain come alive with the intensity of an artistic truth. The dull banalities of everyday life are converted into novelistic experiences. In his search for the little-known people and places of Spain, Cela captures the past, the history of Spain, by dramatizing the fleeting moment, the daily chores, and the humdrum experiences of the people he meets.

Although Cela's books of travels contain the necessary accurate information so as to serve as guides for the places they describe, they create a magnificent effect of fiction. The impression that the reader has is that he is reading a novel. Cela has talent for novelizing the trivialities of life. Even that which seems to have no form, the shapeless daily occurences, the unnoticed gestures and grimaces of colorless people, the dull, abandoned relics of forgotten villages, all are recreated with sympathy.

Cela's books of travels are in effect living texts of Hispanic Civilization. Through the narrations of the author's compulsive journeys the reader pentrates the inner recesses of the Spanish way of life. Cela's obsessive need to explore his country and to search for meaning or form is endless. His incessant quest has no other fulfilment than being. There are no answers, no conclusions. His aim is to experience the totality of Spanish life. In a sense, he recalls the picaresque hero who needs to be contained in the lives of his masters. Cela is inexorably drawn to the existence of his countrymen; his vacuum must be filled with the lives around him.

Cela is not content with being the objective artist who forges life in his study. He is impelled to experience life in the process of being. His intent is to capture the essence of the existence that serves as his model. To accomplish this he integrates himself with his own *materia prima*.

IX. VIAJE A LA ALCARRIA

The first, and possibly the most significant one, of Cela's books of travels is entitled *Viaje a la Alcarria*. Published in 1948, the work explores the little known regions of Zaragoza. Close to Madrid in distance, the towns and villages of *La Alcarria* are seen as shapeless vestiges of a past which at one time exalted order. In the perspective of the aimless present, the past appears as an archaeological relic which may evoke illusory memories but which has little connection with actuality. In the cruel reality of the nineteen forties, disorder reigns in la Alcarria.

In the dissonance of the present with the past, Hispanic life is explored. The intent of the artist is to capture the perdurable values of a people's way of life by dramatizing the incongruity that exists between their sense of history and their physical realm of experience. As epitomized by *el guardia Pérez*, la Alcarria thrives on the recollections of the past.[1] Pride will not permit the inhabitants to face the horror of the present. It is pride—often grotesque in nature—that sustains the dignity of the starving Spaniard.

The baroque structure of Hispanic life in the post-civil war period is examined with sympathy. Cela probes the inner reality of asymmetrical existence with the purpose of capturing its total meaning, and not merely to pass judgment on current events. *Viaje a la Alcarria* is in effect the novelization of the rural Spain which lives ambivalently between the past and the present. Yet, la Alcarria is not torn in its dualistic role; its paradoxical situation gives it charm and dignity.

---

[1] «..., el guardia Pérez es un hombre que vive de recuerdos.» Camilo José Cela, *Viaje a la Alcarria*, Ediciones Destino, S. L., Barcelona, 1954, p. 159.

Even with its occasional ludicrous aspects, it maintains an honorable position. Life flows from its quagmire of contradictions.

Perhaps the most significant utterance of this book is expressed by the innkeeper who says of her house «esto ya no es posada». [2] The *ya no es* becomes the immanent *leitmotif*. But if things are not what they were, neither are they something else. Life here is not in the process of becoming, but rather in the state of not being what it was. The inhabitants of *La Alcarria* have a consciousness of unfulfillment. Their preoccupation is not so much with the future as it is with a vacuous present that does not realize the promise of its past—the townspeople speak not of what is but of what was. They are certain only about the past. Unable to grasp the confusion of the present, which is imbedded in disorder, they recur to bygone days even in negative form for a sense of reality. The identification then, is with a non-existent past.

Within the chaos of contemporary conditions La Alcarria retains a sense of humor about its own failings. There is no despair. Laughter is self-critical, often cruel, but invariably sympathetic. The pride that sustains the Spaniard in an epoch of misery is also his *hamartia*. But in *Viaje a la Alcarria* the tragic flaw brigs tearful smiles rather than terror. The would-be *hidalgo* of *Lazarillo de Tormes* is incarnate in the person of Martín, the traveling salesman who says he is almost a *bachiller*:

> ...algunos compañeros míos son ahora médicos o aparejadores y viven como príncipes. No los trato porque no me da la gana; cuando los saludo quiero ser tanto como ellos y tener mi casa como Dios manda, yo soy muy orgulloso. [3]

Unquestionably, the most pungent remarks are directed against the government, which would like to blame «*los rojos*» for the chaos that exists throughout Spain.

> —Tenemos también un museo de Historia Natural, luego lo verá usted. Está muy desordenado; cuando estuvieron aquí los rojos lo desbarataron todo.

---

[2] *Ibid.*, p. 144.
[3] *Ibid.*, p. 126.

> Desde la terminación de la Guerra Civil habían transcurrido ya siete años. [4]

The mystical qualities of the «glorious movement» of Franco are mercilessly mocked.

> —Es que aquí al amigo Torremocha, ¿sabe usted?, se le tornaron las aficiones con el Glorioso Movimiento Nacional. Cambió el servicio de los santos por el servicio de las armas, y para mí que se quedó entre Pinto y Valdemoro. [5]

For all its claims, for all its love of discipline, the government is unable to restore a sense of order, because *order,* suggests Cela, must emanate from full stomachs. [6] His voice seems like a prophecy for the world turmoil of the sixties.

The acid that flows from Cela's pen centers almost exclusively on the regime which pretends to extoll order. For the people who must endure the hardships of disorganization, frequently utter confusion, the author feels intimate sympathy. Like himself, they are caught in a web of suspicion and mistrust. In a climate of insecurity, only the governmental documents serve to identify the self.

> En el empalme, una pareja de la Guardia Civil le pide los papeles. [7]

In truth, the official papers accentuate the personaless atmosphere of anonymity. «Esto ya no es posada», «¿cómo se llama este parador? —no tiene nombre». [8]

> —Oye: que te estoy hablando. Digo que cómo se llama esta bajada...
> —No tiene nombre.
> A Merche le ayuda una criada zafia y pueblerina, que el viajero no sabe cómo se llama. [9]

---

[4] *Ibid.,* p. 216.
[5] *Ibid.,* p. 158.
[6] «—El estómago es el barómetro del orden.» *Ibid.,* p. 148.
[7] *Ibid.,* p. 157.
[8] *Ibid.,* pp. 144 and 56.
[9] *Ibid.,* pp. 63 and 66.

And yet, amidst the confusion that is contained in anonymity, life flourishes in happiness as in grief. Cela is obviously awed by the indomitable joy for life that exists in *La Alcarria*. Within a social structure that lacks purpose or meaning, life is experienced in its totality. Disorder constricts, but does not limit vital experiences.

> La fonda tiene unas mecedoras que cautivan y unas chicas coloradas, simpáticas, gorditas, que ríen llevando unos cacharros, vaciando un orinal, limpiando el polvo de los muebles, haciendo una cama, fregando el suelo, todo al mismo tiempo, todo en desorden, todo con alegría. Una de las chicas se llama Elena y la otra María. [10]

The author's admiration carries him into an involvement that is novelistic. María likes to read novels. María is a romantic character. The kind words of the traveler touch María's heart. It is Elena who breaks the spell. Elena does not read romantic novels. Elena prefers the reality of a newspaper. And so the traveler's «delightful» thoughts on polygamy are interrupted. [11]

> El viajero sonríe. María se vuelve a la cocina. El viajero está indeciso unos momentos. Cuando llega a la cocina se encuentra a María, hecha un mar de lágrimas, sentada en una banqueta baja al lado del fuego. Elena, que está pelando una cebolla, mira al viajero con un mirar feroz, insospechado. Los ojos le brillan como si tuviera calentura y el seno le palpita con violencia.
> —¿Qué ha dicho usted a mi hermana?
> Su voz, antes bellamente opaca, suena ahora con un timbre metálico odioso.
> —Yo...
> —Usted coge su morral y se va. ¡Como hay Dios! Me debe usted catorce pesetas. [12]

By identifying himself in the third person as *el viajero,* Cela succeeds in giving his person a sense of natural novelistic stature. It is as though there were two Celas, the author and the character.

---

[10] *Ibid.,* pp. 160-61.
[11] «El viajero, mientras oye hablar a Elena y a María, piensa, deleitosamente, en la poligamia.» *Ibid.,* p. 164.
[12] *Ibid.,* p. 166.

In his peregrinations Cela, the character, discovers humor as well as disappointments. Frequently the humor is inoffensive, but at times it is mixed with horror. Undoubtedly, the most comical and pathetic of all characters in this book is don Estanislao de Kostka Rodríguez y Rodríguez, alias «el Mierda». The demented peddler lives in a world of illusions. When recounting his «dreams» don Estanislao arouses laughter.

> ¿Usted ha oído hablar del Virrey del Perú?
> —Sí, mucho.
> —Pues me dejó todos sus bienes. En el lecho de muerte llamó al notario y delante de él escribió en un papel: (Yo, don Jerónimo de Villegas y Martín, Virrey del Perú, lego todos mis bienes presentes y futuros a mi sobrino don Estanislao de Kostka Rodríguez y Rodríguez, alias «el Mierda»). Me lo sé de memoria. El papelito está guardado en Roma porque yo ya estoy muy escarmentado, yo ya no me fío de nadie más que del Papa. [13]

However, when the old man refers to the world of physical experience, the reader shudders with horror, especially if he, too, finds a comic element in the nicknaming of the unfortunate man.

> —Ya le digo. El día de San Enrique del año de la República, me dije: 'Estanislao, esto hay que acabarlo. Eres un desdichado, ¿no ves que eres un desdichado?' Hacía un calor que no se podía aguantar. Yo estaba en Camporreal, me acerqué hasta Arganda y me acosté en la vía. 'Cuando venga el tren—pensé—, Estanislao se va para el otro mundo.' Pero, ¡sí, sí! Yo estaba muy tranquilo, se lo juro, pero era mientras no venía el tren. Cuando el tren asomó yo noté como si se me soltara el vientre. Aguanté un poco, pero, cuando ya estaba encima, me dije: ¡Escapa, Estanislao, que te trinca! Di un salto, pero la pata se quedó atrás. Si no es por unos de la fábrica de azúcar que me recogieron, allí me desangro como un gorrino. Me llevaron a la casa del médico y allí me curaron y me pusieron el mote al ver como tenía los pantalones. Uno de los que me cogieron llevaba la pata en la mano, agarrada por la bota, y no hacía más que preguntar: 'Oiga, ¿qué hago con esto?' El médico se conoce que no sabía qué hacer, porque lo único que le con-

---

[13] *Ibid.*, p. 110.

testaba era: 'Eso se llama pierna, mastuerzo, eso se llama pierna.'[14]

Don Estanislao evokes a profound feeling of sympathy and this bond founded on pity—possibily sentimentality—gives the character a dimension that is lacking in picaresque protagonists. His authentic personality is limited neither to his adopted name nor to that given by his detractors.[15] Don Estanislao de Kostka Rodríguez y Rodríguez, «alias el Mierda», lives in the dualism of a complex existence. His life may be unfulfilled, without direction, but it is not a vacuum. His dreams give his existence content. To be sure, the substance of that content is disproportionate, even grotesque in nature, but it is content nonetheless.

The remarkable aspect of the inhabitants of *La Alcarria* is that they succeed in maintaining a sense of personal reality within the walls of decay that surround them. In a climate of near-nothingness, there is the recollection of an exalted past for which the people wage a battle in fantasy or in the realm of physical reality. Don Estanislao struggles in a sphere of illusions; the priest of the church of the Savior crusades for the restoration of a material object.

>En la parroquia del Salvador hay un púlpito de jaspe, o de alabastro, que debe valer un dineral; ...El cura le cuenta al viajero la última historia del púlpito.
>
>Después de la guerra me costó mucho trabajo encontrarlo. Fue a aparecer en Madrid, en un museo. Al principio no querían dármelo, querían darme otro en vez. Un día me fui con un vecino que tiene una camioneta, me planté a la puerta del museo y les dije: 'Venga ese púlpito, que es mío.' Lo cargué en la camioneta y ahí lo tiene usted.[16]

---

[14] *Ibid.*, pp. 111-112.
[15] In this interpretation I take issue with don Américo Castro, my good friend and teacher, who feels that the authentic personality of don Estanislao de Kostka Rodríguez y Rodríguez, don Basileo de Brazuelo y Murias, is reducible to his alias. «El Vagabundo se deja mecer por la melodía de los nombres profusos —don Estanislao de Kostka Rodríguez y Rodríguez, don Basileo de Bazuelo y Murias—, etiquetas despegadas de un frasco vacío, pues el alias que revela la auténtica persona de don Estanislao de Kostka, es 'el Mierda'.» Américo Castro, «Algo sobre el "Nihilismo' Creador de Camilo José Cela» contained as a separate essay in his study *Hacia Cervantes*, Taurus, Madrid, Febrero, 1960, p. 389.
[16] *Viaje a la Alcarria*, pp. 101-102.

The sense of reality is not always sublime; frequently it is crude and sardonic. Not all inhabitants are capable of transcending the cruelty of the present. And Cela also partakes of the lives of those who cannot escape their miserable existence. Cela's feelings seem to reflect the company of the moment. Whether it be the place of death,[17] or the sight of a virtually waterless streamlet that «drags its poverty»,[18] Cela blends his personality with all that is around him. Sometimes he accomplishes his aim gracefully; in other instances he cannot conceal his prejudices. His integration is humanly imperfect.

> La Escuela de Casasana es una escuela impresionante, misérrima, con los viejos bancos llenos de parches y remiendos, las paredes y techo con grandes manchas de humedad, y el suelo de losetas movedizas, mal pegadas. En la escuela hay—quizás para compensar—una limpieza grande, un orden perfecto y mucho sol. De la pared cuelgan un crucifijo y un mapa de España, en colores, uno de esos mapas que abajo, en unos recuadritos, ponen las islas Canarias, el protectorado de Marruecos, y las colonias de Río de Oro y del Golfo de Guinea para poner todo esto no hace falta, en realidad, más que una esquina bien pequeña. En un rincón está una banderita española.[19]

Cela is better able to share reality, however distasteful it may be, than malicious ignorance. Thus, he is wounded by the students' lack of historical knowledge, which is deliberately distorted by the books of the State. The children learn nothing but empty slogans.

> —A ver, para que os vea este señor. ¿Quién descubrió América?
> El niño no titubea.
> —Cristóbal Colón.
> La maestra sonríe.
> —Ahora, tú. ¿Cuál fue la mejor reina de España.
> —Isabel la Católica.
> —¿Por qué?

---

[17] «—Aquí mataron una vez a uno. El viajero piensa que el sitio está bien elegido, realmente es un sitio muy apropiado.» *Ibid.*, p. 131.
[18] «...un riachuelo casi sin agua que viene arrastrando su miseria...» *Ibid.*, pp. 133-134.
[19] *Ibid.*, p. 173.

> —Porque luchó contra el feudalismo y el Islam, realizó la unidad de nuestra patria y llevó nuestra religión y nuestra cultura allende los mares.
> La maestra, complacida, le explica al viajero:
> —Es mi mejor alumna...
> —¿Cómo te llamas?
> —Rosario González, para servir a Dios y a usted.
> —Bien. Vamos a ver, Rosario, ¿tú sabes lo que es el feudalismo?
> —No, señor.
> —¿Y el Islam?
> —No, señor. Eso no viene.
> La chica está azarada y el viajero suspende el interrogatorio. [20]

And the teacher, buried in the past, remains insensitive to the fraud that is being perpetrated in the present.

The recollection of the immediate past, an intellectual pastime that is witheld from the school children, acts as the instrument of disenchantment in the novelized accounts of life in *La Alcarria*. The visible scars and the unhappy memories of a Civil War constitute the ironic theme of Cela's peregrinatory memoirs. The awareness of the recent holocoust adds a dimension of naked reality as it momentarily bridges the vacuum between history and actuality. The specter of the Spanish Civil War fulfils the role of the chorus in a Greek drama. The author, himself, seems eager to introduce the theme early in the book.

> El viajero trata de hacerse amable, y el niño, poco a poco, vuelve a la alegría de antes de decir: 'Sí, todos tenemos el pelo rojo; mi papá también lo tiene.' El viajero le cuenta al niño que no va a Zaragoza, que va a darse una vueltecita por la Alcarria; le cuenta también de dónde es, cómo se llama, cuántos hermanos tiene. Cuando le habla de un primo suyo, bizco, que vive en Málaga y que se llama Jenaro, el niño va ya muerto de risa. Después le cuenta cosas de la guerra, y el niño escucha atento, emocionado, con los ojos muy abiertos.
> —¿Le han dado algún tiro? [21]

Subsequently the havoc of war is presented by others.

---

[20] *Ibid.*, pp. 174-175.
[21] *Ibid.*, p. 47.

> El viajero baja por unas callejas y se fuma un pitillo, a la puerta de una casa, con un viejo.
> —Parece hermoso el pueblo.
> —No es malo. Cuando había que verlo era antes de la aviación.
> Las gentes de Brihuega hablan de antes y después de la aviación como los cristianos hablan de antes y después del diluvio...
> —Aquí fue donde empezaron a correr los italianos, ¿no sabe usted?
> —Sí, ya, sé.
> —¡Fue buena aquélla! [22]

Throughout the travels of Cela, sometimes more subtly than others, the fragmentary remembrances of the «glorious» uprising of 1936 cast an ominous shadow on life in Spain during the nineteen forties.

But all is not darkness in *La Alcarria*. Here man does not surrender himself completely to external circumstances. He is not reduced to being a pawn of a material machination of «cause and effect». Within his life there reigns a sense of pride which defies the logic of survival. His expression of human dignity is not a romantic gesture; nor is it an expected indulgence in social histrionics. Beyond the realm of social amenities, transcending the consideration of propriety, the behavior of the wretched inhabitants of *La Alcarria* suggests innate majesty. In terms of concrete value, the problem of a *peseta* or two is quite insignificant; translated into personal meaning, the struggle assumes dramatic proportions.

> ...Julio Vacas, alias Portillo, habla con el viajero.
> —¿Es usted aficionado a leer?
> —Sí; a veces leo algo.
> —Pues le voy a regalar a usted dos libros que tengo en mucha estima. Son muy antiguos, son dos libros de sabios. Por ellos no quiero nada: haz bien y no mires a quien. Se los voy a regalar. Son dos libros para la salud; está usted un poco blanco.
> El viajero, mientras el trapero busca los libros, se entretiene mirando las paredes.
> —Aquí están.
> —Pues muchas gracias.
> El viajero busca dos pesetas en el bolsillo.

---

[22] *Ibid.*, pp. 70-71.

> —No; yo estas cosas no las cobro.
> —Perdón, estas dos pesetas no son por los libros, ya sé que valen más, estas dos pesetas son un obsequio.
> —Ese ya es otro cantar. [23]
>
> —Oiga, señora, yo me voy a dar una vuelta por la calle y después me marcharé de Sacedón. ¿Quiere usted darme la cuenta?
> —Sí, señor; aquí la tengo apuntada, son cincuenta y cinco pesetas.
> —No, apúnteme todo, la cena de los dos amigos de anoche y el desayuno de hoy del señor Martín; ya le dije que yo invitaba.
> —Sí, señor, ya está apuntado todo: treinta y seis pesetas las cenas, un duro las camas y doce pesetas los dos desayunos; de servicio le he puesto dos pesetas para redondear.
> El viajero moró la cuenta, por hacer algo, y pagó. Quiso dar un duro de propina y no se lo cogieron. [24]

The vision of man, in conflict or in peace with himself, is predominantly lofty. The circumstances fail to divest man of his human sovereignty. The Spaniard reaffirms his sense of values in face of adversity. The effect may be romantic, but there is a profound sense of reality in the characterization of the Spanish people. In active confrontation with destiny or in passive resignation, it is the image of the person, rather than that of surrounding conditions, that imposes itself on the reader.

The poetic value of the book also rests in large measure on the description of human action or inaction. The theme is life. *Viaje a la Alcarria* begins and ends as a penetrating account of human existence, which is recreated with much of its daily trivialities. The lyrical prose of Cela draws its inspiration from the banal experiences of everyday life. The most common place sights, ignored or easily forgotten by his compatriots, are depicted with literary intensity by the author. Simple words become music. And the song of men is formed.

> El viajero toma por el Paseo del Prado. En los soportales de Correos, la cochambre de la golfería duerme a pierna suelta sobre la dura piedra. Una mujer pasa, presurosa,

---

[23] *Ibid.*, p. 75.
[24] *Ibid.*, pp. 190-191.

el velo sobre la cabeza, camino de la primera misa, y una pareja de guardias fuma aburridamente, sentados en un banco, con el mosquetón entre las piernas. Los misteriosos tranvías negros de la noche portan de un lado para otro su andamiaje sobre ruedas; van guiados por hombres sin uniforme, por hombres de boina, callados como muertos, que se tapan la cara con una bufanda.

—También quisiera decir, que de todo hay en la viña del Señor, la otra verdad:

> Y en todas partes he visto
> gentes que danzan o juegan,
> cuando pueden, y laboran
> sus cuatro palmos de tierra.
>
> Nunca, si llegan a un sitio,
> preguntan a dónde llegan.
> Cuando caminan, cabalgan
> a lomos de mula vieja,
>
> y no conocen la prisa
> ni aun en los días de fiesta.
> Donde hay vino, beben vino;
> donde no hay vino, agua fresca.
>
> Son buenas gentes que viven,
> laboran, pasan y sueñan,
> y en un día como tantos
> descansan bajo la tierra. [25]

But if death made itself felt at the beginning as an inexorable part of living at the end of the narration there is more breath of life. The mention of death does not escape us, but now it is more subdued. As dusk falls, life is rekindled.

El traqueteo del coche le produce sueño. Da dos cabezadas y reclina su cabeza sobre el hombro de don Paco, el médico, el hombre que sonríe siempre con una sonrisa velada, levemente, lejanamente triste.
Al llegar a la plaza de la Hora, el viajero se despierta.
—¿Ha descabezado usted un sueñecito?
—Sí, señor; usted perdone que me haya apoyado en su hombro.

---

[25] *Ibid.*, pp. 29-30.

En la plaza los hombres charlan en grupo y las chicas pasean rodeadas de guardiaciviles con gorrito cuartelero, de guardiaciviles jóvenes que las piropean y las enamoran. Unos niños juegan a pídola en una esquina, y unas niñas, en la esquina contraria, saltan a la pata coja. Cruza algún señorito de corbata, y ríe una muchacha airosa; muy mona, calzada con fino zapatito de tacón alto.
Por el monte del Calvario cae la noche sobre Pastrana.

Por la plaza de la Hora,
se pone el sol.

Enlutada, una señora
vela al Señor.

Suena triste una campana,
con suave amor.

Por el cielo de Pastrana,
vuela el azor.

Empiezan a encenderse las luces eléctricas, y el altavoz de un bar suelta contra las piedras antiguas el ritmo de un bugui-bugui.
Don Mónico, don Paco y el viajero se meten en el casino a tomarse un vermú con aceitunas con tripa de anchoas...[26]

Literary and physical experiences are interwoven in the wanderings of Cela. The sense of total reality does not discriminate between fact and fancy, history and legend. Indeed, that which is *believed* to have happened is as true as that which was witnessed. In the last analysis, belief attains a greater sense of validity than empirical experience. The artistic integration of human sensation is but a reflection of Cela's theme, «The Spanish way of life». If the technique seems diffused or disparate in *Viaje a la Alcarria*, if the book is not carefully contrived so as to have a semblance of order, it is because the author seeks to reflect not merely in content but also in form the nature of his subject.

In the intermingling of literature and life, there are delightful moments in *Viaje a la Alcarria*. In one instance, Pío Baroja, the man

---

[26] *Ibid.*, pp. 222-224.

of flesh and blood, appears as a virtual fictional entity to the characters, whose own reality rests on artistic creativity. The reference to Baroja as a *señorito* is particularly amusing. Cela is not merely reporting on the wealth of the frugal Basque writer; instead, he is recreating the nebulous image of Baroja, who exists as a phantom in the minds of the peasants. Thus, Baroja, like Cela himself, becomes a character in the book without losing his physical identity as a man. There is, of course, profound irony, almost a lament, in the description of the peasants' reaction to the name. In the nineteen forties Baroja, living in isolation and under governmental persecution, had been reduced to practical anonymity.

> Tendilla es un pueblo de soportales planos, largo como una longaniza y estirado todo lo largo de la carretera. En este pueblo es donde tiene un olivar el escritor don Pío Baroja, para poder tener aceite todo el año.
> El viajero habla con las chicas de la taberna.
> —¿Conocen ustedes a Pío Baroja?
> —No, señor.
> —¿Y no saben quién es?
> —No, señor, tampoco.
> La madre, que ha salido de la cocina, interviene.
> —Sí, hijas, sí; ese señor es el señorito de la Eufrasia, es el que ha comprado ese terreno del sendero de Moratilla, el que está dando con el del tío Pierdecarros.
> —¡Ah, sí! Pero ese señor no viene nunca por aquí, debe ser ya muy viejo; el secretario dice que es un señor muy importante, de lo más importante que hay. [27]

The people of *La Alcarria* dwell in an atmosphere of hearsay and namelessness. Even concrete personalities are reduced to abstraction. Without a sense of historical reality and without consciousness of hope for the future, the inhabitants pursue their daily chores of living aimlessly. They wander through their existence as though the act of living were less of an effort than dying. They are as half asleep and half awake. Only a consciousness of personal reality prevents them from being submerged in the deluge of chaotic anonymity.

---

[27] *Ibid.*, pp. 198-199.

X. EL GALLEGO Y SU CUADRILLA

El Gallego y su cuadrilla is a literary fantasia of travels that take place in the creative imagination of its author. The original date of publication remains some what of a mystery. The years 1949 and 1951 are included in the first edition, each year in a different part of the book, to be sure.[1] Curiously, the 1955 version, in which the author alludes to the confusion, carries the description of «primera edición». It would seem as though Cela's publishers, in their own limited possibilities, were trying to express the author's image of chaotic life in Spain.

El Gallego y su cuadrilla is deliberately grotesque. In some instances the book has a semblance of continuity; in other cases, there is no connection between preceding and succeeding content. Some of the selections could be categorized as essays; others are short stories. The majority of the titles defy definition. Whereas part of the book deals with abstract dehumanized topics, a good portion is devoted to the analysis of fascinating extra-social characters, some possibly real, some completely imaginary. Often, if a selection appears to be gaining traditional form, it is abruptly discontinued. Better that it should hang in midair! In this case, the intent of the artist is to express lack of harmony, to depict a shapeless world.

---

[1] «'El Gallego y su cuadrilla', en su primera edición, fue un librillo breve y humilde, impreso en Toledo y plagado de erratas, en rústica y generosamente prologado por el investigador Rodríguez-Moñino, que reunía veintiún apuntes y que se vendió al asequible precio de tres duros. En el lomo marca la fecha de 1951, pero en la portada interior, en la que presume de madrileño, es dos años más viejo. ¡Misterios del mundo editorial!» Camilo José Cela, *El Gallego y su Cuadrilla,* Ediciones Destino, S. L., Barcelona, 1955, Prólogo, p. 9.

Although this book lacks the note of total despair so prevalent in *Los Sueños* of Quevedo, there is mixed with the realm of awake experience a dream-like quality of horror. Here the reality of the travels rests on man's ability to recall a nightmare, as though half asleep and half awake. Thus, a consciously believable incident is intertwined with an essay or relation that is hallucinatory. And just as the reader becomes resigned to a nightmarish ambient, he is brought back to a situation which relates to his own physical surroundings in time and place. In the traditional Spanish novel, from Cervantes to Baroja, we could still distinguish between physical and imaginary reality, even when we placed as much value on the latter as on the former. Now, we are confronted with a world which has become a receptacle for human experiences, seemingly without feeling and without a sense of discrimination.

The book begins on a theme of abstraction. The title of the first selection is *Un Pueblo*. But there are no people in the *pueblo* that is Castile. We have a picture of barrenness as we see Spain's most significant province «naked».[2] Along with this harshness we are presented with a brief description of poetic delicacy. «...un vientecillo de siglos se estremece ligeramente sobre las altas copas de los árboles, delante de la iglesia.»[3] There is even a rational observation, worthy of an academician, regarding Castile's basic economic problem. «Lo único que le falta al pueblo es agua, agua para dar y sobrar;...[4] The second episode finds the author in Cebreros, a village of Castile. There are literary allusions to Santa Teresa and Antonio Machado, but the key word which recalls the recurring theme of drought has reference to a dog. «Un perro pasa, el rabo entre piernas, la lengua seca, husmeando distraídamente sabe Dios qué suerte de rastro perdido.»[5] Yet, the essay does not end on this note, for Cela resorts to the dream element of life to escape the agony of living. And so he dreams of water. «El escritor, un poco contagiado ya, entorna los ojos y sueña con un Cebreros con agua, con

---

[2] «...la sequía de cuatro siglos, esa sequía que desnudó a Castilla...» *Ibid.*, p. 17.
[3] *Ibid.*, p. 19.
[4] *Ibid.*, p. 17.
[5] *Ibid.*, p. 21.

un Cebreros feliz,... Cuando Cebreros tenga agua —que la tendrá algún día...» [6]

Doña Concha, the principal figure of the subsequent vignette, is also barren, like her land. Again the theme of sterility is dramatized. True, she has an «ascetic» sense of her condition, but she «suffers», nonetheless. In her moments of dreams she wishes herself a widow. These are dreams that occur while she is awake. She feels some compunction for her thoughts, and since she understands her role in society, the delightful thoughts are transferred to another event, when pigs are slaughtered in honor of San Martín and the smells of blood and *anis* are intermingled. Although the last sentence assures us that tomorrow will be another day, we know it will be just as today. As Cela says in the following pages, «y el día empezó a tomar, poco más o menos, el aire de todos los días». [7]

Possibly the most amazing feature of these vignettes is the author's ability to touch upon different human situations in a few pages. Impressions of horror, humor, and sentimentality are interwoven in one event as though they all comprised an unending and uneven solidarity. In the description of *La Romería*, Cela recreates the life of a family which, for all its absurd vicissitudes, inspires compassion. By themselves, the usual occurrences of an ordinary holiday are banal, but taken together and sprinkled disproportionately with horror and pity, they form a picture that is as believable as it is fantastic.

> —¿Y te acuerdas de cuando aquel señorito se cayó, con pantalón blanco y todo, en la sartén del churrero?
> —También me acuerdo. ¡Qué voces pegaba el condenado! ¡En seguida se echaba de ver que eso de estar frito debe dar mucha rabia! [8]

Calling the father «el cabeza de familia» is obviously ironical. He does not have much of a voice in family affairs. The poor man tries hard to be the head of his entourage but his success is questionable.

> El cabeza de familia, para recuperar el favor perdido, le preguntó al hombre:

---

[6] *Ibid.*, p. 22.
[7] *Ibid.*, p. 29.
[8] *Ibid.*, p. 27.

>—¿Están frescas?
>—¡Psché! Más bien del tiempo.
>—Bueno, deme cuatro.
>Las gaseosas estaban calientes como caldo y sabían a pasta de los dientes. Menos mal que la romería ya estaba, como quien dice, al alcance de la mano. [9]

The author's attitude toward the father's pusilanimity reveals itself in these words.

>La familia llegó a la romería con la boca dulce; entre la gaseosa y el polvo se suele formar en el paladar un sabor que casi se puede masticar como la mantequilla. [10]

And suddenly we have a group of soldiers singing songs of the Civil War though, as the author reminds us, the war has been over for eleven or twelve years. The scars remain. The soldiers, themselves grotesque vestiges of the past, are playing the part of drunken heroes. They are neither drunk nor heroic. «Los soldados no estaban borrachos, y a lo más que llegaban, algunos que otros, era a dar algún traspiés, como si lo estuvieran.» [11]

The children, on the other hand, are described with delicate compassion. At times Cela is tenderly sensitive to children's feelings.

>El niño empezó a llorar por dentro con una amargura infinita. Los ojos le escocían como si los tuviese quemados, la boca se le quedó seca y nada faltó para que empezase a llorar también por fuera, lleno de rabia y de desconsuelo. [12]
>El niño, que iba de la mano del padre, se calló como se calló su padre. Los niños, en esa edad en que toda la fuerza se les va en crecer, son susceptibles y románticos; quieren, confusamente, un mundo bueno, y no entienden nada de todo lo que pasa a su alrededor.
>El padre le apretó la mano.
>—Oye, Encarna, que me parece que este niño quiere hacer sus cosas.
>El niño sintió en aquellos momentos un inmenso cariño hacia su padre.

---

[9] *Ibid.*, p. 34.
[10] *Ibid.*, p. 34.
[11] *Ibid.*, p. 35.
[12] *Ibid.*, p. 36.

—Que se espere a que lleguemos a casa; éste no es sitio. No le pasará nada por aguantarse un poco; ya verás como no revienta. ¡No sé quién me habrá metido a mí a venir a esta romería, a cansarnos y a ponernos perdidos!

El silencio volvió de nuevo a envolver al grupo. Luisito, aprovechándose de la oscuridad, dejó que dos gruesos y amargos lagrimones le rodasen por las mejillas. [13]

As the day ends, the three adults, the husband, the wife, and the mother-in-law, are overtaken by an ominous silence which heralds a storm, a storm which may or may not abate.

La hija levantó la cabeza y la miró; no pensaba en nada. El yerno bajó la cabeza y miró para el plato, para la rueda de pescadilla frita; empezó a pensar, procurando fijar bien la atención, en aquel interesante expediente de instalación de nueva industria.

Sobre las tres cabezas se mecía un vago presentimiento de tormenta... [14]

In *Una Jira* there is an ironical description of Hispanic cruelty as applied to the crudity of nicknames.

Las señoritas Esperanza, Olguita y Marisol eran las tres altas y recias, las tres gruesas y algo bigotudas, las tres morenas y bien plantadas. A la mayor le habían vaciado un ojo de una pedrada que le dieron en un carnaval, hace ya años; desde entonces, en el pueblo, y como para compensar, le pusieron de mote *La Tuerta*. A la segunda la dejó un novio viajante que tuvo, a la puerta de la iglesia; la empezaron a llamar *la Plantá*. A la tercera, que le quedó la boca torcida de una enfermedad, la llamaban, simplemente, *la Tonta*. Los que las bautizaron, como puede verse, eran un dechado de caridad y de tierno corazón. [15]

Whereas Cela alludes to the unkindness of this baptism, he partakes of the harsh humor and also laughs at the girls.

---

[13] *Ibid.,* p. 39.
[14] *Ibid.,* p. 41.
[15] *Ibid.,* pp. 42-43.
[16] *Ibid.,* pp. 43-44.

> ...a Marisol, *la Tonta,* no se le ocurrió mejor cosa que beberse una botellita que ponía por fuera 'Salsa del Condado de Worcester', y a la pobre le entró semejante colapso al vientre, que por poco se nos va. [16]

> ...lo malo fue que no se pudieron sentar en todo el tiempo porque los trajes, que eran muy finos, se les hubieran puesto perdidos. [17]

There is one brief instant of sentimentality as Cela speaks of the effect that a song has on «la Tuerta». «A *la Tuerta,* sin saber por qué ni por qué no, le dió un vuelco el corazón en el pecho. A veces pasan cosas algo raras.» [18]

Other episodes, often completely unrelated to one another, deal with life and death, war, charity, and the ridiculous aspects of the Franco regime. Cela probes into Spanish life by means of every conceivable theme that makes an impression on his stream of consciousness wanderings. Some of his topics are reminiscent of the traditional *cuadros de costumbres* of the 19th century. But here the treatment is undeveloped. Frequently we are left with a fractional impression. It isn't that Cela is against certain institutions as were the *costumbristas.* The author is not passing judgment; he is merely experiencing the nightmare that is Spain. In fact, he is enjoying his dream. If the vision brings tears, it also carries laughter.

> Hay unos momentos de presentido silencio y la puerta giratoria, como una noria verbenera, lanza a los novios dentro del Café. Primero entra la novia —cuarenta años, treinta arrobas, innúmeros granos y mantilla a la española— e inmediatamente se cuela el novio —edad indefinida, veinticinco onzas, bigote a lo John Gilbert, smoking y síntomas de avitaminosis.
> La madrina está triste; probablemente le aprietan los zapatos. [19]

The irony that pervades the glimmers of Spanish life is indefinite. One cannot be sure if it contains a predetermined proportion of bitterness and sympathy. Possibly Cela himself is unaware of the ratio.

---

[17] *Ibid.,* p. 44.
[18] *Ibid.,* p. 44.
[19] *Ibid.,* p. 50.

«El pueblo tiene cinco cafés: uno, el Ideal, incluso bien instalado, casi limpio,...»[20]

«Al Café de la Luisita iban los jóvenes, y los viejos que no se resignaban a serlo».[21] The first observation is caustic, the second almost sentimental.

In the fanciful impressionistic nightmares of Camilo José Cela, the subject matter, as well as the characters, meet or clash in the disparate fashion of a dream that one is having while he is not quite asleep. From the range of imaginative characters, we have the image of partial reality as flesh and blood personalities are mingled with imaginary ones. The author, himself, as Camilo the *Gallego,* appears as the grotesque protagonist in a tale of a would-be bullfighter. Possibly every *aficionado* has envisaged himself a master in the ring, but here the image is almost a burlesque of such a dream.

> *El Chicha, Cascorro* y Jesús Martín andan siempre juntos, y cuando se enteraron de que al *Gallego* le había salido una corrida, se le fueron a ofrecer. *El Gallego* se llama Camilo, que es un nombre que abunda algo en su país. Los de la cuadrilla, cuando lo fueron a ver, le decían:
> —Usted no se preocupe, don Camilo, nosotros estaremos siempre a lo que usted mande.[22]
> El toro estaba con los cuartos traseros apoyados en el pilón, inmóvil, con la lengua fuera, con tres estoques clavados en el morrillo y en el lomo; un estoque le salía un poco por debajo, por entre las patas. Alguien del público decía que a eso no había derecho, que eso estaba prohibido.[23]

Under the title of *Baile en la Plaza* there is one of Cela's favorite recurring themes, blood. Again, it appears as the symbol of life, and in this selection which dwells on the many aspects, moral and esthetic, of the fluid, there is the mixture of joy and sorrow, life and death.

In the forging of pathetic characters, Cela's irony is benign; in the description of institutions the laughter is harsh, frequently destructive. «A la tertulia iba un muchacho muy jovencito que había querido estudiar para cura, pero al que tuvieron que echar del Semi-

---

[20] *Ibid.,* p. 51.
[21] *Ibid.,* p. 52.
[22] *Ibid.,* p. 58.
[23] *Ibid.,* p. 60.

nario porque estaba medio tísico y a lo mejor acababa contagiando a todo el mundo;...»²⁴ But if the Church knows what it wants and what is best for it, the people are unconscious of the world around them. For them, life drifts meaninglessly.

> Por el pueblo —por uno de esos milagros que ocurren— no había pasado el tiempo desde García Prieto, y la República, la guerra civil y la revolución la conocían un poco de referencias, con no mucho más detalle que al cólera de Egipto, o la guerra de China, o la inmigración judía de Palestina...
> ...a lo mejor un poco con la felicidad del hombre que no tenía camisa —y se dejaba llevar por sus fuerzas vivas vitalicias,...»
> Vivía por la misma razón que la tierra gira, que el sol se pone a diario y que los animales nacen, crecen, se reproducen y mueren.²⁵

In the unfinished impressions of life, no one escapes appearing ridiculous, least of all, the artist. Thus, Fermín de la Olla, unable to find himself in any endeavor, degenerates into poetry. His lack of success in his new venture is less painful; he thrives on distorted imagination for the creation of his poems and for his image of himself. His life is anything but hazardous; it is banal.

> La vida del pueblo seguía monótona y apacible, como la vida de una doncella, y la vida de Fermín de la Olla, 'la azarosa vida de Fermín', como le gustaba oir, marchaba paralela a la vida del pueblo, como en las carretas el buey de la izquierda camina paralelo al buey de la derecha...²⁶

Not so pathetic is the description of the political situation, the regime of Franco. Here governmental persecution is the object of mockery.

> Como el director de la revista le contestó con evasivas, y no le publicó en los catorce meses que estuvo suscrito mas que dos sonetos, Fermín de la Olla, harto de la burguesía y de la explotación, se hizo comunista, pero no comunista

---

[24] *Ibid.*, p. 73.
[25] *Ibid.*, p. 78.
[26] *Ibid.*, p. 83.

de Stalin, cosa que no estaba bien vista en su pueblo, sino comunista de Tito, que se sabía menos lo que era. [27]

By means of ridicule, the reader becomes aware that the tentacles of the Spanish government reach far beyond the range of tradition and reason.

>—Y por último, ¡la rosa!
>—Oiga usted, ¿de qué es símbolo la rosa?
>Celedonio Montesmalva puso los ojos en blanco.
>—La rosa es símbolo de la luz, del goce y del amor.
>El sensato intervino:
>—Oiga, ¿y usted cree que eso lo dejará pasar la Censura? [28]

Even as Cela creates a caricature of himself as «Zoilo Santiso un escritor la mar de tremendista», government censorship occupies the lowest possible level of absurdity.

>—¡Quememos los libros de Zoilo Santiso!—decían los muchachitos que no habían leído a Zoilo Santiso, pero que se fiaban del buen criterio de sus mayores—. ¡Guerra a Zoilo Santiso, escritor asqueroso y tremendista! ¡Guerra! [29]

The image of death is no less bizarre than that of life.

>Don Belisardo falleció, como su padre, a consecuencia de un grano. Los granos, a veces, cuando se enquistan y son de orden maligno, pueden precipitar a un fatal desenlace, en literatura, ya se sabe lo que significa: palmarla y quedarse tieso como un palo de escoba. [30]
>Deogracias murió aplastado por un camión de pescado una noche de romería, en que volvía de un pueblo próximo a Mondoñedo con el fagot a cuestas, y cuando le trajeron hecho totalmente una oblea... [31]

---

[27] *Ibid.*, p. 82.
[28] *Ibid.*, p. 99.
[29] *Ibid.*, p. 101.
[30] *Ibid.*, p. 116.
[31] *Ibid.*, p. 121.

The deformity of humanity is continuous; the cessation of life magnifiies the grotesqueness of man's existence. There is neither pity nor nihilistic joy before the decay of the flesh. The world moves as a senseless orgy.

The disparate vision that Cela expresses of life becomes manifest in his style, which ranges from the poetic to the coarsest possible treatment of human experience. Cela's crudity gives no warning. It is contained out of proportion in circumstances that do not logically demand unrefined language. Thus, the first part of a statement may be linguistically totally unharmonious with what follows.

> Hay quien nace con afición a la Geografía, y quien con la vehemente vocación de hurgarse las narices...
> ...y todos dijeros que a la Marixa la había amamantado una loba, cosa más probable que atribuirle el asunto a los pechos de Emeteria, que ya no era moza cuando la carlistada. [32]

The author's consciousness of lack of order in style as in sequence is deliberate. Thus, when an episode is about to become too orderly or too logical, he calls a halt to the narration quite abruptly.

> Uno del público: —Oiga, ¿hasta cuándo va a seguir usted?
> El inventor de estas invenciones: —Hasta que ustedes quieran; esto es como el cuento de la buena pipa. [33]

Whereas some of the selections are sheer fantasy, there are those that recall the virulent pen of Mariano José de Larra. The distinct feature of Cela's critical «*artículos*» is that they retain a sense of humor or perhaps it is that Cela has no illusions about changing the Spaniard, as Larra did.

¡Ah, Las Cabras! presents us with a long absurd —but amusing— speech in which the goats are blamed for the ills of Spain. It is they who eat the trees, hence no forests, hence no rain, hence no cattle, hence no meat, hence no will to work, and so on. All this in a two page speech in a *tertulia*.

In *Un invento del joven del principal* Spanish humor, cruel and crude, destroys genius. A young inventor is crushed by the obscene interpretation of his machine.

---

[33] *Ibid.*, p. 207.

—Oiga usted, Filo: ¿le ponemos el orinalito a la cafetera?
—llegaron a decirle un día.

La pobre Filo Pérez, acongojada por las opiniones que suscitaba su cafetera, llamó un día a su sobrino Baltasar y le dijo:

—Mira, niño: la gente es inculta, ya sabes tú, y se ríen de nuestra cafetera.

—¡Anda! ¿Y por qué se ríen?

—Pues ya ves... Dicen que si la cafetera parece que está haciendo aguas.

—¡Vaya por Dios! ¡No había caído yo en eso! ¿Y dicen todos lo mismo?

—No, hijo; no dicen todos lo mismo. Unos dicen que talmente está haciendo aguas menores, y otros, más soeces, dicen que no, que lo que parece es que está haciendo aguas mayores.

—¡Qué horror! [34]

—Oye, Baltasar, hijo: ¿por dónde sale el humo?—preguntó con voz trémula.

El joven Baltasar Ruibarbo se dió cuenta y creyó desfallecer.

—Por detrás, tía, por detrás—respondió con un hilo de voz—. He tenido que aprovechar el tubito de la cafetera...

La tía y el sobrino estuvieron una hora larga en silencio, cabizbajos, abatidos, como bajo el peso de una pena profunda. [35]

In another selection the *Vuelva Ud. mañana* of Larra becomes *Quizá Pasado Mañana* and in *Sebastián Panadero, Marcas y Patentes* Cela seems to be echoing the cry that Spain is destined to remain primitive. «Sí; verdaderamente, esto de ser inventor en España es un mal oficio. España es un país muy susceptible, y aquí los inventores se mueren de hambre». [36]

Although Cela's humor may turn into pathos when the object of ridicule is an individual who is struggling to exist as someome he cannot become, it is hilariously comical when it is directed against American advertising. The inventive satire is as devastating as it is

---

[34] *Ibid.*, p. 196.
[35] *Ibid.*, p. 197.
[36] *Ibid.*, p. 168.

amusing. The supposed incident is related by a funeral director, don Juan de Dios, who in the author's words «olería un poco a muerto.» [37]

> Ya no es verdad eso de que el buen paño en el arca se vende. Mi industria, por lo menos, necesita mucho de la propaganda. En el Congreso de Funerarios, que se celebró en Nueva York, se llevó el primer premio de publicidad una casa que llegó a vender mucho haciendo famoso un *slogan* que decía: 'Señora, caballero, ¿por qué se empeña en seguir viviendo cuando la casa Tal, por tantos dólares, puede organizarle a usted un entierro bellísimo y sensacional?' [38]

The fantastic content of *El Gallego y su cuadrilla* is almost indescribably heterogenous. The subject for inspiration may be an innocent child, six years of age, an executioner, or sensational criminals. In *Vocación de Repartidor*, for example, Cela writes with delicacy, indeed with sentimentality of a six year old child who willingly suffers the agony of physical pain so that he may be accepted as a friend by a group of older children.

> —¿Y, entonces, por qué vienes con éstos?
> Robertito miró al señor con unos ojos tiernísimos de corza histérica...
> —Es que es lo que más me gusta.
> Por aquel misterioso planeta, aquel séptimo cielo de las vocaciones que no se explican, corría una fresca, una lozana brisa de bienaventuranza. [39]

In *Un Verdugo* we have cruelty of a virtually absolute nature. The only expression of tenderness is contained in the criminal, and at that, it is egotistical.

> Estando ya atado al palo, *el Gallego* le dijo a Mayoral:
> —Espérate un poco.
> Y volviéndose al director de la prisión, le dijo:
> —Pido a usía que me suelten las manos un minuto.

---

[37] Naturally, the association of the Allmighty Creator and Death is in itself a significant revelation of the meaninglessness of life.
[38] *Ibid.*, p. 140.
[39] *Ibid.*, p. 150.

> El director hizo una seña a Mayoral y Mayoral soltó las manos al *Gallego,* quien sacó un pañuelo de seda del bolsillo y se lo puso alrededor del cuello.
> —Es que eso está muy frío.
> 'Eso' era el corbatín de hierro. Verdaderamente, en Burgos, en enero, de madrugada y en semejante trance, debe de estar todo bastante frío. [40]

In the account of murderesses, who recall the deeds of Pascual Duarte,[41] Cela reveals himself more indulgent and in a better humor than when he wrote his first novel. Inured to cruelty for the sake of cruelty, the author is able to find —and express— humor in the basest of men's actions.

> El Juan González, amador rendido, no sabiendo bien dónde se metía, cumplió al pie de la letra los deseos de su novia y se presentó en la casa armado con dos pistolas, una escopeta y un cuchillo de dos filos: casi lo bastante para levantar una partida y armar la marimorena...
>
> Sebastiana, al verlo en tierra, lo mató también—y ya van tres—, se vistió con sus ropas, sacó un caballo de la cuadra y se echó al monte, como suele ser costumbre: igual que el torero Tragabuches, uno de los siete niños de Ecija...
>
> Ante el patíbulo, Sebastiana del Castillo se mostró arrepentida y murió confesada y con el ánimo abatido. Menos mal. [42]

Of course, in the last quoted passage the object of laughter is not so much the criminal, herself, as the highly esteemed ceremony of the last rites.

As the reader reaches the end of the book, he is overwhelmed by the gallery of characters and topics that he has experienced. *El Gallego y su cuadrilla* is a collection of embryonic impressionistic vignettes whose common foundation is that they all emanate from the

---

[40] *Ibid.,* p. 267.
[41] «La joven Sebastiana, que murió de veinte años no cumplidos, nació en Javalquinto, un pequeño pueblo de Sierra Morena, y fue un típico Pascual Duarte, un ser hecho para atropellar y destrozar todo lo que oliese a vivo.» *Ibid.,* p. 269.
[42] *Ibid.,* pp. 270-71

cerebrum of Camilo José Cela. In terms of motif, each is incomplete unto itself.

The intensity of the book is such that the end comes as a welcome relief. The partitive sensations that are produced in the reading of disconnected material is oppresive. To the reader accustomed to a sense of harmony or continuity, the effect is one of shock. *El Gallego y su cuadrilla* defies traditional classification of genre. The theme is life or anything that pertains to human existence, thoughts, art, dreams, nightmares. Woven together with ambivalent —often completely disparate— emotions, the only logic is the demonic logic of literary creation. In the last analysis it is Cela's artistic personality that holds together, however precariously, the selections of this book. After all, they are his hallucinations.

XI. DEL MIÑO AL BIDASOA

Del Miño al Bidasoa (1952), constitutes a delightful interlude in the separatistic art of Cela. More than any other of his books of travels, this one recalls in spirit the wanderings of our literary Lord, Don Quijote de la Mancha. It might have been entitled, «Nuevas andanzas y aventuras del caballero de la triste figura». As did his predecessor, here the vagabond has a companion to share his quaint experiences. Their relationship, built on instinctive sympathy, is as beautiful as that of Don Quijote and Sancho though it operates on a plane of equality. The vagabond and his friend, the Frenchman Dupont, serve each other. There are no masters, no squires. In the twentieth century adventures there are only people.

Possibly the most striking aspect of *Del Miño al Bidasoa* is its dominant note of peace and serenity. Life remains without direction, but there is no turmoil. In this area of Spain, from Santiago de Compostela, to Asturias, to San Sebastián and finally to Irún, Cela recreates a world in which the people are at peace with the land. Without reason, without understanding nor seeking to understand why, the characters of this book rejoice in their existence. With occasional intermingling pathos, joy and good humor reign in *Del Miño al Bidasoa*. It is as if this work were the «día de fiesta» of Cela's writings.

Created with fervent sympathy, in a mood of contemplative admiration, the vagabondage of Cela attains moments of lyrical beauty in the description of the locale, «donde la tierra acaba y la mar, que no acaba jamás, comienza a herir y a enamorar».[1] In the narrative, however, the novelistic technique prevails. Sympathetic irony brings

---

[1] Camilo José Cela, *Del Miño al Bidasoa*, Editorial Noguer, S. A., Barcelona, 1952, p. 27.

together the Quixotic and the Sanchonian realms of reality. But here one cannot predict who will play the role of the dreamer and who will unmask the dreams. At different times a character may play both roles. In the last analysis, everyone has his moments of madness, and his moments of disillusionment. However, the transvestitism of ideals or perspectives is achieved through a process of benign irony.

Although life continues to lack definite form in *Del Miño al Bidasoa*, there is a sense of well-being in the suspended animation in which human existence finds itself. It would appear that Cela, the author, were now more secure about the shapeless world he depicts. In the earlier books of travels he insisted on paiting disproportionate symbols, on emphasizing disparate reality. In short, he was struggling to reveal to us his experience of disproportion, his affirmation of the rupture of harmony. In this work, Cela contents himself, not feeling the need to preach, with recreating life in its inexplicable—and perhaps unjustifiable beauty. And Cela, as a literary character, partakes of the joy of living.

The preponderance of celebrations which abound with good food and the flow of wine serves as a background for the travels of the vagabond and his companion. There are countless expressions of friendship, numerous incidents of recognition and gratitude which result in joyous celebrations. In comparison with the earlier books of travel, life here is prosperous. No one appears to be hungry. And this in itself represents good tidings. No greater enemy hath the Spanish land than hunger.

To the absence of hunger as a *leitmotif* we may add the exclusion of horror as a theme in *Del Miño al Bidasoa*. Aside from its intrinsic aesthetic value, in terms of an historical understanding of Cela's works, the significance of this book rests largely on the banishment of certain topics which normally characterize the content of Cela's actual and imaginary wanderings. Here there is no hunger, no horror; in fact, there is no evil. Every character is sympathetic; all circumstances are surmountable, or at least bearable. Free of acrimony, the author can laugh at the pedestrian order of bourgeois vacationers while he seeks beauty in the disorder of nature. *Del Miño al Bidasoa* may be viewed as a relief. Certainly, it represents a prominent departure from what might have appeared to be a pattern of human depravity. Although still without purpose, lacking any sense of logic, here the vision of man is essentially triumphant. In spite of his inability to make decisions, man goes forward, conquering the land.

The element of surprise is overwhelming. The anticipation of a sudden change in the mood of *Del Miño al Bidasoa* is unfulfilled. The reader remains in suspense, fearing that at any moment he may experience the chords of dissonance, so prevalent in the symphony that comprises Cela's art. But there are no disparate incidents; the strings of his instruments do not break. The melody carries forth a tune of life which alternates between the realm of experience and the creative plane of imagination. The dualism is proportionately balanced even though it is never resolved. The effect, however, pleases the senses.

Beyond a state of indulgence or passive resignation, Cela elects to live the land and taste of its fruits. Leaving aside the bitter herbs that also flourish in the earth that is Spain, the vagabond dedicates himself to the recreation of an existence which, for all its shortcomings, has its joys and pleasures. Nowhere was Cela so happy as in the description of this particular region. No longer alone, in the company of another compatible traveler, he finds social acceptance. The land now tolerates vagabonds; it is a more kind and fertile land. Though not completely satiated—Cela's need to explore his earth must remain insatiable if he is to live as an artist—the author suggests in the last pages of this book that perhaps he is prepared to withdraw. Very possibly, he was already contemplating refuge in Palma de Mallorca.

Even before the book begins, in the quotation from Micer Francisco Imperial, there is the suggestion that Cela's perspective will be benign and delicate.

> Era en (la) vista benigna e suave
> e en color era la su vestidura
> çenisa o tierra, que seca se cave,
> barba e cabello albo syn mesura.
>
> Traía un libro de poca escriptura,
> escripto todo con oro muy fino,
> e començaba: El medio del camino
> e del laurel corona e çentura.
>
> Micer Francisco Imperial
> (Desyr a las syete virtudes.)

In the singularly brief introduction—Cela seems eager to relate his fortunate peregrinations—the author explosively expresses his vision of the Spanish land, which is described as inexhaustible, eternal, and protean. «He aquí, lector amigo, otro libro de viajes, otras páginas nómadas, otras visiones y otras andanzas a través de los paisajes españoles, de los inagotables y eternos y proteicos paisajes españoles.» [2] The author further refers to the pleasure that this particular journey afforded him and utters the hope that the reader, too, will be amused. Finally, he admonishes the critic to aproach literary technique in whatever form he chooses but to do it with sympathy not in the despair of tedium. Even sadness is worthy of love. «De lo que se trata es de que esa aguja no llegue a marcar el cuadrante sin remisión del hastío, esa tristezza senza amore de que se nos hablaba en el xix italiano, eso tan desesperador y tan huérfano.» [3]

The vagabondage of *Del Miño al Bidasoa* begins with a religious theme as the author joins a peregrination in honor of Santa Marta de Ribarteme. In this somber spectacle of life and death, the image of the coffin is transposed to evoke beauty and hope.

> Como el vagabundo no tiene ni amigos ni parientes ni, por no tener nada, ni un perrito que le ladre, lleva, por entre las madreselvas y los tojos del camino, su ataúd a la cabeza, igual que una cesta de frescas manzanas de esperanza. [4]

The word *ataúd* is rendered powerless as it is transformed in a figure of speech that suggests «fresh apples of hope». And soon the earthly enjoyment of life manifests itself in the delights of eating and drinking.

> El vagabundo, después de la procesión, comió y bebió todo lo que pudo, se templó las carnes, que halló más aliviadas, y, con los últimos solecicos sobre el verde horizonte, se echó otra vez al camino, ... [5]

Having made his entrance on the stage as a Don Quijote, in quest of spiritual values, Cela ends up as Sancho in the first episode, satiating his physical needs.

In the second chapter, as he approaches Santiago de Compostela, Cela integrates himself in the narrative as a literary personaje and as

---

[2] *Ibid.*, «Introducción».
[3] *Ibid.*, «Introducción».
[4] *Ibid.*, p. 15.
[5] *Ibid.*, p. 16.

the man of flesh and bones. «—Pues, sí señor caminante..., que de esta casa, gracias a Dios, no salió seco ningún amigo de don Camilo...»⁶ With superb irony, the setting oscillates between the realm of human experience and the plane of fantasy, or in a manner of speaking between the flesh and the spirit. Naturally, Cela makes it clear that he knows more about the flesh than he does about the spirit. «El Cuco y el vagabundo, ante sus tazas de vino, hablaron, según las viejas reglas de todo lo humano y de casi todo lo divino.»⁷ His prayers further attest to his concern for the body. «...se detiene en el vetusto Padrón, a rezar por su alma y por sus dolientes carnes ante la piedra santa—el Pedrón—...»⁸ It is precisely in this second episode, in the sanctuary of Cuco's tavern, that Cela acquires the identity of a temperate ironical vagabond, a kind of philosopher with a sense of humor about the incongruity of life, and a sentimentality for the past. As in the case of Don Quijote, the pilgrim becomes a knight-errant in the alcoholic atmosphere of an inn.

The author sings his praise for Rosalía de Castro in romantic terms as he heads toward the altar to pray. He cannot remain too long in a state of abstract ecstasy and as he is about to commune with the lord, he very ironically raises the question of miracles.

>—Y vamos de milagro...
>—Sí, señor, que milagros los hay a mares, pero lo que pasa es que no nos damos cuenta.⁹

Once he is on his knees, in the posture of spiritual devotion, it is the flesh, his flesh and the flesh of humanity in desultory motion, that inspires his supplications.

> El vagabundo, ya no en la Iria-Flavia, de rodillas ante el altar que se levanta sobre el Pedrón, reza por sus amargas carnes y por las carnes amargas de todos los vagabundos de la tierra, de los hombres de todos los pelos, todas las alzadas y todos los mirares que viven y mueren por los caminos del mundo, esos caminos que nunca se sabe bien adónde llevan.¹⁰

---

⁶ *Ibid.*, p. 18.
⁷ *Ibid.*, p. 18.
⁸ *Ibid.*, p. 18.
⁹ *Ibid.*, p. 19.
¹⁰ *Ibid.*, p. 19.

And again, the traveller returns to the house of Cuco «el hombre que no dejaba salir seco a ningún amigo de sus amigos».

In Santiago de Compostela, the shrine of Spain, a breakfast of «aguardiente con rosquillas» and a good cigar break the sentimental spell of the journeyer [11] After all, his reason for praying is to give thanks for being kept alive, «a dar gracias al Santo por conservarlo vivo...» His experience of life knows no bounds; the past meets the present as he extolls the well-proportioned restraint that characterized the epic heroes of Spain. Ancestral grandeur is evoked in form of feminine coquetry. «La señora sonrió, casi sin ser notada, con un mohín de ancestral y bien medida coquetería.) [12] Here there is an element of *mesura;* it is the past!

At the tomb of the apostle there is an air of serenity, but the vagabond remains confused. [13] The desire of the traveler in this oasis is to fill his soul with water because he knows that the cruelty of life, the sun, will again dry and deteriorate his provision.

> El vagabundo—¡no es por nada!—quiere coger en Compostela su abundosa provisión de agua, quiere llenarse hasta el borde las cantimploras del alma, los mismos vasos que el sol secará sin remisión en cuanto vuelva a caminar la heroica, la cruel meseta. [14]

Unable to resolve his spiritual conflicts, the author feasts in the manner of his ancestor Pardo de Cela, «el héroe de todas las leyendas gallegas». [15] Finally, he visits the church of Santa María where the problems of souls are also dealt with in a physical manner.

> Por el claustro de Santa María, detrás de un caballero templario vestido de fantasma, corre con un palo en la mano un monaguillo tartaja con el pelo de la hermosa color de la zanahoria.

---

[11] "En la taberna del Asesino, el vagabundo, sentado a la mesa de dos besteiros de los montes de Rebordechao que se le hicieron amigos, desayuna aguardiente con rosquillas, se fuman sus cigarros de tabaco de la vega de Padrón...» *Ibid.*, p. 21.

[12] *Ibid.*, p. 21.

[13] «El vagabundo, después de su confusa y piadosa oración, sale a la calle a empaparse, avaramente, con el orballo, que cae lento como una bendición: igual que un viejo y complicado amor.» *Ibid.*, p. 22.

[14] *Ibid.*, p. 22.

[15] *Ibid.*, p. 22.

>—¿Adónde vas, muchacho?
>—Ya lo ve, mi señor, a dar dos palos a un alma en pena...
>Por encima de las cabezas del monaguillo y del vagabundo pasa, casi invisible, un ánima en desgracia. [16]

Although Cela is not without irony about the sense of disproportion that exists between appearance and actual reality, he seems more kindly disposed than ever to recreating the land that is truly his, Galicia.

> El vagabundo... sale silbando un son de muñeira... a meterse en tierra pontevedresa por Puente Ulla, en el valle del Hórreo, más allá del Pico Sagro, que presume más de lo que abulta. [17]

In the ancestral setting of his youth, the totality of life is experienced joyfully. In the compenetration of the spirit and the flesh, legend and reality, there emerges a new tenderness for human existence. His pilgrimage to Galicia, in particular, affords him a benevolent perspective of life. Instead of obliteration, we have coexistence.

> En Bandeira, el vagabundo se encuentra con su hermano de la andante orden de los caminos, que le invita a rezar una salve y a tomarse dos tragos de vino en el monasterio de San Lorenzo de Carboeiro... [18]

And the most trivial traditions of Galicia, acquire fresh meaning, and beauty.

> En Lalín el vino no se pide por tazas sino cuncas, por hermosas cuncas en cuyo blanco vientre de loza caben media docena de tazas bien cabidas. [19]

True, Cela does not remain enchanted for long. Suddenly he is awakened to the comical aspects of myth as he undertakes the search for the birthplace of his illustrious ancestors.

> ...un tío al que Dios Nuestro Señor hizo santo, quizá porque hubo la suerte de nacer el día del Apóstol del año en que los franceses se asustaron por las calles de Madrid. [20]

---

[16] *Ibid.*, p. 22.
[17] *Ibid.*, p. 25.
[18] *Ibid.*, p. 25.
[19] *Ibid.*, p. 25.
[20] *Ibid.*, p. 26.

On the other hand, the essence of reality often rests on the legendary treatment of history, and bears are presumed to have existed because the names of places attest to their existence.

> El vagabundo, que no ha visto osos en todo el camino, piensa que en algún tiempo, quizás no lejano, debió de haberlos, dados los nombres con los que se encuentra. [21]

The element of irony does not completely remove the spirit of credulity on the part of the author. Cela doubts and believes at the same time. He is especially reverent about the past. The confusion of the present drives him into the security of the past.

> Al pie del monte Alegre, por el vetusto y noble caserío de Orense, el vagabundo piensa que ha de entrar con tanta calma como respeto, con tanto aplomo como recogimiento.
> Porque Orense es villa vieja y de noble origen, ciudad levantada a buen golpe de cincel sobre piedras de ilustre antigüedad. [22]

The disproportion of the present finds escape and solace in the symmetry of the past. Thus, we have an essay on «Un puente romano de cumplidas proporciones». In this eulogy of harmony there are poetic glimmers of Cela's momentary integration with monotonous orderliness.

> Entre los juncos de la orilla, las ranas se adiestran en su monótona gimnasia mientras cantan, con su mala voz, su poco variada letanía. [23]

Yet, within this conscious submission to a sense of bygone proportion, the author maintains his perspective of the purposelessness of his own times. The contemporary Spaniard merely lives.

> Hay quien piensa que Anfíloco, el troyano, fue el fundador de Orense. Hay quien piensa que fueron los celtas. Hay quien piensa que fueron los suecos, quienes se lavaron sus frías carnes en las calientes aguas de la *Warmsee*. Hay quien

---

[21] *Ibid.*, p. 26.
[22] *Ibid.*, p. 26.
[23] *Ibid.*, p. 29.

piensa que fueron los romanos, que tradujeron la Warmsee por Aquae urentae. Hay también quienes, como Benitiño do Chao y el vagabundo, no piensan nada.
—¿En qué piensas?
—En nada, no estaba pensando en nada. [24]

The commentary on Hispanic life may appear to be captious but underneath the critique there is manifest assent. In effect, Cela exclaims «so be it», and he proceeds to integrate with the situation. In terms of the philosophy of Ortega y Gasset, in this work Cela becomes the man and his circumstances. «Como al día siguiente es fiesta —no importa qué fiesta—...» [25] Whatever the celebration, the author, like his fellow countrymen, partakes of it. In the same vein, he is made aware of the ephemerality of politics and the dominant value of religion. «Mondoñedo, que perdió el gobernador civil, sigue conservando el obispo.» [26] The author feels comfortable in the serene ambiance of Mondoñedo because it is peace that he seeks. Until then he had been unable to find tranquility in his life. «El vagabundo, que ama la calma por encima de todas las cosas de este mundo...» [27]

Although Cela delves into the history or legend of the regions he visits, his primordial preoccupation is with life in the present. Even while appearing to be mesmerized by the folklore that envelops his ancestry, his concern is for the living.

> El vagabundo..., prefiere apagar su sed por las tabernas, por las murmuradoras, por las rumorosas, por las vivas tabernas mindonienses—o mondoñedinas, que es más claro—, donde se sirve el vino con los viejos rituales que vieron morir a golpe de hacha al mariscal don Pedro Pardo de Cela, el hombre que se enamoró de un paisaje y murió por él. [28]

The key word is *vivas*. If history is to have any meaning for Cela, it must be found as a burning vestige among the living.

For Cela, Spain is a thirst that cannot be quenched. Supported by opposite pillars, illusion and despair, the author continues his unending

---

[24] *Ibid.*, p. 28.
[25] *Ibid.*, p. 38.
[26] *Ibid.*, p. 39.
[27] *Ibid.*, p. 39.
[28] *Ibid.*, p. 41.
[29] *Ibid.*, p. 42.

wanderings, knowing that total possession is impossible. Yet, he must fufill his insatiable desire to recreate Spanish life.

> Y el vagabundo..., pensando en vanos y angélicos revolares, en los revolares que se irá *bebiendo,* con tanta ilusión como desesperanza, por el prolongado cáliz de los caminos de España, de los caminos cuyos pasos, igual que las arenas de la mar, son incontables. [29]

The words *ilusión* and *desesperanza* constitute the motivating extreme poles that come together in *Del Miño al Bidasoa*. In this work the literary incitement is made up of illusion and despair. Both forces exist in sympathetic ambivalence. Often, in the past, the merger had produced monstrous images. Perhaps the ingredient of illusion was lacking in force.

There is a deliberate sense of unbalance in the creations of Cela, who seems to be fascinated by the mystery of disproportion. His *ars poetica* rests on the indecipherable.

> Al vagabundo se le ocurre que éste sería un arranque bonito para un cuento sin fin, un cuento eterno y misterioso, sin pies ni cabeza, como deben ser todos los cuentos. [30]

His morbid fear is to be classified and catalogued; he wants so much to be irreducible as an artist. [31]

Del Miño al Bidasoa abounds with undeveloped novelistic bits of human existence. The author strives to quench his thirst for «drinking Spain» by novelizing the dreams and illusions of the people he meets. However incongruous, the characters are draw with sympathy. Their dreams may be intellectualy absurd, but translated into art form, they acquire charm and dignity.

> —¿Y no tienen ustedes familia?
> —Sí, señora, que tenemos mucha y muy buena, y Dios dispone las cosas de forma que en cada pueblo nos topemos con una hermana de los pobres y de los caminantes.

---

[30] *Ibid.,* p. 49.
[31] This is made quite clear in his «prefatorial retort» to Olga Prjevalinsky in *El Sistema Estético de Camilo José Cela,* Editorial Castalia, Valencia, 1960. («Prólogo de C. J. C.»)

La señora sonrió con un gesto elegante y un poco triste y coqueto.
—¿Cómo yo?
—Pues, sí, por ejemplo. [32]

Mostly, the humor evokes kind feelings. Thus, in the mixture of charity and opportunism on the part of an innkeeper, we have the picture of a very real man, not totally good, but not completely bad.

El tabernero, después de cobrar su primera jarra, tomó confianzas y les invitó a la segunda. Dupont y el vagabundo, después de bebérsela, pensaron que mejor sería pagar la tercera, y el tabernero, en agradecimiento, les convidó a la cuarta. [33]

The tale of the celibate, Tristán Balmaseda, punctuated with humorous comments, constitutes a neo-picaresque episode, that recalls the experiences of Lazarillo de Tormes with *el escudero*. The name, itself, of the saloon keeper (his place is not an inn), Tristán Balmaseda, combines the opposite elements of distinction and banality. While *Tristán* has literary qualities, there is a commonness about *Balmaseda*. His physical impairment, too, lacks the dramatic experience it suggests.

El Tristán Balmaseda estaba picado de viruela y movía con dificultad uno de los remos.
—¿Un paralís?
—No, señor, un camión de pescado.
—¡Vaya! [34]

In the pompous unconcious irony of Tristán Balmaseda, there is revealed the soul of a man who struggles to conform to the image that he has of himself.

The description of Tristán Balmaseda's life follows the migratory pattern of his name, from the chivalric to the ordinary. The grandiose first statement or illusion is soon brought down to the realm of cruel experience. «—Un servidor de ustedes, señores, vino al mundo..., en un hogar que hubiera sido tranquilo si mis padres se llevaran mejor, ...» [35] Thus, «que hubiera sido tranquilo» meets its doom as it

---

[32] *Ibid.*, pp. 118-119.
[33] *Ibid.*, p. 117.
[34] *Ibid.*, p. 129.
[35] *Ibid.*, p. 129.

is unmasked by «si mis padres se llevaran mejor». And so it is with his illusions of serving a «noble lady» who turns out to be a «procuress». «... allí entré al servicio de una dama... que las malas lenguas la llamaran alcahueta.»[36] Her kindness would have been impressive indeed, had there been enough for Tristán to eat, too.

> En su casa nunca faltaba un bocado que llevarse a la boca y no era culpa de ella, y tampoco se lo echo en cara, que en vez de un bocado no hubiera habido dos para que yo me aprovechase del segundo. ¿Otra copita?[37]

Although the celibate appears to be hypnotized by his autobiographical account, he maintains a sense of reality about himself and the two vagrants, who costitute his audience.

> ...ya sin preguntar lo que sabía, sirvió otras dos copitas... ¡Caray, cómo soplan ustedes, hermanos! ¿Quieren ustedes cambiar a vino?[38]

Through irony, Tristán Balmaseda relates to the present. Even the divine sphere becomes a part of the stage. «—Aquí en Torrelavega hubo, en mi vida, de todo como en la viña del Señor, ...»[39] And the audience answers in kind. «Dupont y el vagabundo... escuchaban como embobados el incesante parlar de Tristán Balmaseda e intentaban aprender, por amor al arte, la lección que no había de servirles para nada.»[40] The author and his companion are thoroughly invested with the technique of the story-teller. They have become momentarily permeated with the descending dualism of Tristán Balmaseda.

Cela's joyful integration with the land in *Del Miño al Bidasoa* has an air of extravagant merrymaking. However trite or insignificant the occasion, a sense of happiness adorns life. Here the vision of Spain is expressed in nearly euphoric terms. The ordinary sight of young girls bicycling or the appearance of herrings arouses ecstatic eulogy. More significant still is the author's need for company. Dupont has become a pillar of support for the author, who had previously shunned

---

[36] *Ibid.*, p. 230.
[37] *Ibid.*, p. 130.
[38] *Ibid.*, p. 131.
[39] *Ibid.*, p. 131.
[40] *Ibid.*, p. 132.

company. «...llamó a Dupont, que se estaba lavando los pies en un arroyo, para animarle a proseguir el camino.»[41] Cela's *piropo* upon viewing some young ladies on bicycles evokes a sincere lyrical image.

> Dupont y el vagabundo, al verlas pasar igual que mariposas, se descubren como saludando, reverenciosos, a una bendición del cielo o, lo que es muy parecido, a una punta de corzas solteras en libertad.
> —¡Que Dios las bendiga!
> —Sí, que a nosotros ya se ha dignado bendecirnos con el premio de verlas pasar.[42]

His sensuous description of a food, which occupies a rather low position in the hierarchy of delicacies, gives it aristocratic stature.

> Los arenques de la tabernera de La Marina, negros, sabrosos y de buen tamaño, son unos arenques exquisitos, unos arenques soberanos, unos arenques para días de fiesta, unos arenques que, si fuera costumbre darlos en las bodas, no faltarían en ninguna boda lujosa, en ninguna boda rumbosa, postinera y abundante.[43]

The migration in the tale of the celibate had been from the apparent noble to the ordinary. Here the order is reversed.

Even in Santander, which is filled with bourgeois vacationers, the author retains a sense of humor. Ejected from a fashionable hotel, Dupont and Cela react with supreme understanding.

> —Por ser la primera vez, no los echo a ustedes con un par de patadas en el trasero.
> —Muchas gracias.
> —No hay de qué.[44]

They consider with equanimity the possibility of being bathed because sometimes the forceful process is followed by the consumption of soup.

> —Hombre, amigo señor Dupont, a propósito, ¿usted cree que no nos cogerán los municipales para cortarnos el pelo y

---

[41] *Ibid.*, p. 138.
[42] *Ibid.*, p. 137.
[43] *Ibid.*, pp. 138-139.
[44] *Ibid.*, p. 141.

> darnos un baño con desinfectante? En algunas ciudades dan también un plato de sopa. [45]

And prostitution does not have the air of tragedy it had in *La Familia de Pascual Duarte*. It is viewed here as just another possibility for living, in the same calm ironical manner as potential sainthood.

> Toñito tiene un hijo que es practicante y una hija que gana muy buenos cuartos en Barcelona, haciendo la carrera...
> ...se llama Austregisila Marimón y Cebollada y tiene una casa de huéspedes en Astorga que fundó con los dineros que le dejó en herencia un tío cura que tuvo y que iba para santo. [46]

In Cela's two previous books of travels, *Viaje a la Alcarria* and *El Gallego y su Cuadrilla*, the author, as a literary character, seemed to drift aimlessly along with the others. In *Del Miño al Bidasoa* the element of free will affirms itself as an inalienable right of man. Even in a terrain of definitely limited possibilities, there are several roads and the author enjoys the luxury of knowing that he can choose. «...el vagabundo... se divierte reservándose siempre hasta el fin el derecho a elegir.» [47] No longer do Cela and his people appear as immobilized specters of humanity. In any case, however lowly the choice, the vacationers may resolve their doubt by becoming «crabs» or «lizards». «...dudan entre bañarse en la playa, como los cangrejos, o darse a andar por sus callejas y sus barrios, como los lagartos, ...» [48] Naturally, in the earlier books of travels, water was lacking. Here it is plentiful. The choice is to bathe or not to bathe. The natives of the city conserve their inimical views toward the precious liquid, as does the author: «...mientras los forasteros beben agua, se llenan el buche de vino para no sentar malos precedentes.» [49] Dupont believes that the frivolous use of water reduces man to the animal level. «...que los cristianos se anden bañando a todas las horas como los perros de aguas.» [50] At any rate, when there is choice, there is laughter.

---

[45] *Ibid.*, p. 142.
[46] *Ibid.*, pp. 144-145.
[47] *Ibid.*, p. 149.
[48] *Ibid.*, p. 154.
[49] *Ibid.*, p. 157.
[50] *Ibid.*, p. 155.

Cela is conscious that the landscape evokes literary experiences of the traditional *costumbrista* novel of the 19th century, «paisaje que huele a vieja novela costumbrista...»,[51] but his own experience of the land and its people is more nearly novelistic in the manner of Cervantes, and the Galdós of *Fortunata y Jacinta*.[52] As an example of this mature artistry, we have the dialogue between himself and Dupont. The plane of myth and the realm of human possibilities come together, without destroying each other. In the last analysis, myth prevails, even though its absoluteness has been permeated with ironical questioning.

> —¡Ya lo creo! ¡Un gran horror! Desde entonces, el 'Palestina' navega infatigablemente las aguas de aquellas costas, siempre con su mujer en llamas a bordo...
> —¿Y no acaba de arder?
> —¿Cómo quiere usted que deje de arder si es un espíritu?[53]

If the vagabond punctures the sphere of myth by asking whether the ship hasn't burned out yet, Dupont mocks empirical reality by reminding his friend that the subject in question is a *spirit,* an essence beyond the power of reason. And finally, the Frenchman reminds the Spaniard that myth is an article of faith with the force of law, and that God supports fantasy.

> —Y es ley de la mar y artículo de fe entre marineros, que el que no cree en los navíos fantasmas con ellos habrá de cruzarse alguna vez en su vida, por castigo de Dios...[54]

It is ironic in itself that a Frenchman should be upholding faith, while a Spaniard champions reason.

In moments of contemplation and introspection the autor seeks to elevate himself and his land to a chivalric plane. Calling himself a *vagabond,* he defines the word in lofty terms. «Marco Polo, que también era un vagabundo, aunque un vagabundo de primera, ...»[55] He

---

[51] *Ibid.,* p. 152.
[52] By the Galdós of *Fortunata y Jacinta* I mean the mature Galdós, the superb writer dedicated to the recreation of Hispanic life. This is not the captious and partisan Galdós of *Doña Perfecta.*
[53] *Ibid.,* p. 157.
[54] *Ibid.,* p. 159.
[55] *Ibid.,* p. 163.

strives to characterize his region as good and prosperous. «—Y además, el país por el que vamos nada tiene de malo y da lo bastante para que podamos vivir y casi prosperar con lo que a los otros les sobra después de haber vivido y prosperado.» [56] And the slightest privileges of life are seen as benedictions. «—Y también es una bendición de Dios poder mirarse en las aguas a cada paso, y contar una a una todas las gaviotas de la costa, ...» [57] Cela has not completely lost his vision of life as a meaningless drift but now he feels that such a position represents *one* possibility. The key word in the ensuing quotation is O. «—O a vivir ya toda la vida que nos quede sin movernos, ...» [58]

Out of a world of disparities is born coexistence. Opposite forces need not obliterate each other. Thus, a generous man can be cruel, and at one and the same time he may be possessed of fierce kindness, as is Nicolás, the bartender.

> —El vino lo cogéis de esta cuba. Si lo cogéis de otra o si empezáis a cantar, a armar escándalo o a vomitar, por éstas que son cruces que os echo a punterazos. ¿Enterados? [59]

Purity of feelings is an abstraction. Cela no longer searches for order in his time; in fact he finds it tedious when it occurs, as among the vacationers. «Los veraneantes suelen ser gente metódica, bien organizada, puntual, llena de orden...» [60]

Cela had known in his earlier travels that he was looked upon as an oddity, but in his anger to depict a shapeless Spain, he was little concerned with public opinion. Here, however, he wishes to relate to his countrymen, his audience. He makes an effort to explain his compulsive need to travel and «drink of Spain», even though he has scarce hope of being understood.

> Bien cierto es, y ni a Dupont ni al vagabundo se les oculta, que esto de andar y andar sin ton ni son, de un lado para

---

[56] *Ibid.*, p. 164.
[57] *Ibid.*, p. 164.
[58] *Ibid.*, p. 165.
[59] *Ibid.*, p. 168.
[60] *Ibid.*, p. 170.

> otro y no más que por el puro gusto de andar, es ciencia, o arte, que el sedentario ni se explica ni entiende demasiado. [61]

The author senses the abyss that exists between his literature and his readers. The children, in the role of an audience, think of him as being from another planet.

> Los niños, cuando el vagabundo los saluda, ponen un gesto de sorpresa, le miran como si fuera un ser caído de otros mundos, y no le contestan. [62]

But Cela does not quarrel with their position. He has become more tolerant, more understanding, and more resigned to his anomalous situation. His voice may still clamor in the desert, but in the complex civilization that he lives, it becomes a whisper, and often one of acquiescence. Naturally in the process of intellectual assimilation, he endeavors to maintain his right to dissent. «...la industria es algo que tiene escasa defensa, algo que hay que tolerar porque es necesario y útil para los demás, pero no por ninguna otra razón.» [63] His willingness «to speak the language» of his contemporaries is dramatized in his conversation with a devout woman of Bilbao. The stubborn provincialism of the lady is vexing and amusing at the same time. The humor is quite serious.

> —Oiga, señora, ¿dónde está el puerto?
> La señora se detiene y ensaya un gesto extrañísimo.
> —¿El puerto? No, señor; aquí no hay puerto.
> —Perdone.
> Cuando el vagabundo se va, la señora lo llama.
> —Aquí lo que hay es ría. ¡Como no pregunte usted por la ría...!
> El vagabundo tiembla un poco.
> —Pues, sí, la ría. ¿Hacia dónde cae la ría?
> La señora abrió sus apagados y piadosos ojos.
> —¿Cae?
> —Sí, ¿hacia dónde está?
> —Está por ahí abajo; vaya usted todo seguido.
> —Muchas gracias.

---

[61] *Ibid.*, p. 169.
[62] *Ibid.*, p. 175.
[63] *Ibid.*, p. 175.

Al vagabundo, bien claro estaba, no le entendían en Bilbao. [64]

Cela has not surrendered completely to the serenity and sobriety of the environment. He conserves some doubt about the reality of attaining peace. He expresses his fears graphically. «—¡Parece como si por aquí fuera todo demasiado fácil! ¡Parece como si estuviera todo preparado para que nos sacudiésemos, nada más llegar, las pulgas de la preocupación y de la congoja!» [65] Further on, he and Dupont, so as if to show their inability to conform to their society, resort to picaresque tricks of flattery and deceit to fleece a victim of his money.

> Tan elegantemente hace usted las cosas, señor padrino, que hasta en lo que da, estos cinco duros... sabemos agradecérselo a usted como si fueran el doble, diez duros... [66]

But they do not remain in this rapacious state for long. Soon, they display a great sense of charity for each other and further on painfully admit that the disproportion of life can have its rewards. They come to the realization that life can have its moments of fairy-tale beauty. «—Sí, ¡qué le vamos a hacer!, la vida, a veces, es bella y amable como las figuras que los artistas pintan en los tapices.» [67]

Cela's phobia is rationalization; the obsession to encase life as though it were a mathematical formula fills him with odium and revulsion. He considers himself in vital need to live the land that surrounds him, «es hombre que no nació para vivir nunca demasiado lejos del polvo de los caminos», but he is deeply offended when asked «why» or «where is he going». He deems such probing utterly irrelevant and senseless.

> —¿Adónde van ustedes?
> Dupont y el vagabundo pensaron que la pregunta era una insensatez de tomo y lomo, una insensatez que se las traía. [68]

In this book, disorder leads us to beauty and truth. It almost gives us a sense of proportion. As expressed in the life of the multi-

---

[64] *Ibid.*, pp. 176 and 177.
[65] *Ibid.*, p. 188.
[66] *Ibid.*, p. 193.
[67] *Ibid.*, p. 202.
[68] *Ibid.*, p. 206.

faceted poet, «...que unas veces se llama don Rafael, otras don Gabriel y otras aún don Juan», madness becomes delightfully novelistic. The poet, whom we might remember as don Rafael if it were Friday («—Bueno, bueno, muchas gracias por todo, don...» «—Rafael; hoy, viernes, pueden ustedes llamarme don Rafael.»),[69] is created in the image of the early Don Quijote. In the 20th-century version, however, the process of mutation lacks definite form. Cela continues to refer to him repetitively as don Gabriel, or don Juan, or don Rafael, even on Friday.

In the indefiniteness of the poet's identification, there are the absolute qualities of charity and nobility of character. We do not really know who he is, but we do know that he is a good man, who succors wandering poets and other indigent travelers. Moreover, he serves as an inspiration for sympathetic self-analysis. His quest for identity inspires in others a need to have a perspective of the self, in terms of dreams as well as facts. That is to say, the poet radiates his madness.

Through the creation of Don Gabriel, or don Juan, or don Rafael, the author mirrors his own personal frustrations. With a sense of humor about his own feeling of isolation, Cela, himself, becomes the object of ridicule.

> —Y además, según dicen, es un poeta muy admirable, un poeta de esos que hacen versos y después publican libros con los que van escribiendo.
> —Ya, ya. ¿Y es conocido?
> —¡Uf! ¡La mar de conocido! ¡Es uno de los poetas más conocidos que hay! ¡Yo creo que lo conocen hasta en el extranjero!
> El vagabundo se quedó pensativo.
> —¡Pues ya es mérito! [70]

Further on, Dupont reminds the vagabond that if poets were not eccentric, they would be as commonplace as they, two, are.

> «Si no tuviesen manías, no serían poetas, serían como usted y como yo, gente del montón.» [71]

---

[69] *Ibid.*, p. 221.
[70] *Ibid.*, p. 222.
[71] *Ibid.*, p. 222.

The ironical Cela mercilessly flays himself, but he displays understanding for the dream qualities of his characters. There is pathos in the bartender's description of la Encarnita, the pretty crippled girl, «who lives as best she can». In spite of his sense of reality about the girl's occupation, the bartender idolizes her, and elevates her to the realm of Dulcinea del Toboso. «...el chico del mostrador veía a la Encarnita como una lejana e imposible Dulcinea.» [72] In the last analysis, he is no less mad than our good poet. Indeed, neither are the vagabond and Dupont who, upon leaving San Sebastian, steal a book from the home of their benefactor, don Rafael, or don Gabriel, or don Juan, to give to la Encarnita as a parting gift.

Irún is the final stop for the vagabond and his French companion. Here, where Spain meets France, they must part. Dupont returns to his native land and Cela, having drunk of Spain, but still thirsting, knows not where to go. He only knows that he must continue to search for the «why» of life. «...Dupont y el vagabundo tenían que buscarse su porqué para seguir viviendo...» [73] Naturally, to find the «why» would be the end of the search and the search is life, itself. The terrifying aspect of the last chapter is the suggestion that Cela was contemplating refuge in a place that is far away from the heart of Spain. It is quite possible that already Cela was thinking of retirement or exile in Palma de Mallorca.

Del Miño al Bidasoa is to Cela's books of travels what *La Colmena* is to his novels. It represents the highest literary point of his published wanderings. Only one year separates their publication. And in spirit, they are practically identical. Both of these works represent a turning point in the artistic life of Cela. The early Cela, whom we might designate as the Cela of the nineteen forties, writes in anger. His despair emanated from his inability to find order in the world which he inhabited. The Cela of the nineteen fifties, the mature Cela, still retains a keen sense of despair, but it is now tempered with an appreciation of illusion. Having established the existence of disproportion, Cela learns to enjoy life in its fullest disorder. It is not a sense of logic but rather man's ability to transform chaotic reality into a fanciful dream that elevates man to a sphere of well-being. In

---

[72] *Ibid.*, p. 224.
[73] *Ibid.*, p. 230.

the Spain of the forties dreams were only of the past, the present was a nightmare.

The acceptance and appreciation of Hispanic life on the part of Cela, the artist, does not remove the personal disappointments that the author continues to experience with the state of affairs in the Spain of Franco. But here we are concerned with the artictic vision of Cela, not his views as a person of flesh and blood. Obviously, there is no definite schism in the two positions and the prejudices of the man often manifest themselves in his art. Unquestionably, Cela has moved from a posture of despair and disillusionment to one of resignation and understanding. At any rate, no longer can he be so certain about the misfortune of living. Perhaps it is happiness after all.

> El vagabundo, otra vez solo como siempre andara, no supo si llegó a sentirse desgraciado, acongojadamente desgraciado, o feliz, inmensamente, luminosamente feliz. [74]

In the style of *La Colmena,* in *Del Miño al Bidasoa* there is a «census of characters» following the end of the adventures. Cela wants his characters remembered. His peregrination has made a profound impression on him. In part he is pleasing himself in the recreation of persons and places (there is also a geographical census); in some measure, he is attempting to interpret to his audience. At this point of his literary career, Cela still entertains the hope that he might have a sympathetic audience in Spain. When *Mrs. Caldwell habla con su hijo* appears the following year, he becomes conscious of the insurmountable chasm that exists between him and his Spanish readers, and proceeds to dramatize that abyss. [75]

Even Cela's works which might be designated as non-pessimistic (though not completely optimistic), like *La Colmena* and *Del Miño al Bidasoa* for example, lack sympathetic reception in Spain. For one thing, Cela had already been categorized as a brutal pessimist in the minds of the critics and the censors. Often the distinction between the two is merely semantical. Moreover, his meager audience—it has not been popular in the Spain of Franco to admire Cela as a writer—felt offended by the nakedness of his portrayal. In other

---

[74] *Ibid.,* p. 235.
[75] See chapter on *Mrs. Caldwell Habla con su Hijo.*

words, the Spanish readers would not look beyond the real circumstances of hunger, prostitution, and general depravation that characterize Cela's literary milieu. Perhaps, the setting seemed more of a photograph than a painting, and the audience a stage. And by the time that *Del Miño al Bidasoa* appears, the die is cast. Although hunger and depravity (prostitution is not so offensive in Spain) do not play a role in this book, the image of the early Cela has been firmly implanted in the minds of his contemporaries.

XII. JUDÍOS, MOROS Y CRISTIANOS

With the publication of *Judíos, Moros y Cristianos* (1956), Cela establishes himself as a historian, and in particular as a partisan of Américo Castro's concept of Spanish history.[1] The regions explored in this book of travel are aptly described by the sub-title, «Notas de un vagabundaje por Segovia, Ávila y sus tierras». The study of «Castilla la Vieja» spans parts of two decades. Begun in 1946, it is completed, amidst interruptions of other writings and wanderings, in 1952. It is finally written up in Mallorca, the new residence—and sanctuary—of Camilo José Cela. Quite naturally, the book expresses the complexities of the time and space it embraces.

Judíos, Moros y Cristianos has many faces. As a work of fact, it may be viewed as an erudite historical analysis, with a geographical guide, of «Castilla la Vieja». As a work of fiction, it is a collection of likely and unlikely tales of Ávila and Segovia. As a study of Cela's literary development, it is the book which reveals to us, almost simultaneously, the two Celas, the angry Cela of the forties and the understanding, mature Cela of the fifties. Taken in its aesthetic totality, the book is a detailed factual account of history interwoven with the fancy of the moment.

The prologue to *Judíos, Moros y Cristianos* constitutes a critical essay on the traditional historical and geographical treatment of «Castilla la Vieja» as well as a declaration of intent on the part of the author. While analyzing the morass of scholarly confusion that reigns over the region which is the heart of Spain, Cela proposes to give his account a sense of proportion by means of literary interruptions which will permit the reading of the book in portions, beginning at any point.

---

[1] The title itself is revealing but also see note 32, chapter II.

In the ironical words of Cela, disorder becomes the key to order. «...el vagabundo ha procurado ordenar su libro con un placentero desorden que permita leerlo a trozos y abrirlo por cualquier lado.» [2]

While pretending to be amazed by the inconsistencies that exist in the works that presume to be factual descriptions of «Castilla la Vieja» (actually, he expects no harmony in any aspect of life), Cela succeeds in appearing as a scholar whose discoveries constitute a new truth. Naturally, he loudly protests that he does not wish to be didactic, but in protesting too much, he reveals his inner desire to be acclaimed as a man of wisdom. Thus, after pleading that his work not be construed as «educational», he asks that neither be he taken for an ignoramus. «Como contrapartida, el vagabundo ruega a su lector que no piense que, de una manera forzosa, estas líneas están escritas por un ignorante». [3]

In his prologue, Cela speaks as a professor. We have before us now the image of a man who is the director of a learned journal, *Papeles de Son Armadans*. He has not completely lost his impertinence, but neither does he flaunt it. There is a sincere attempt to reach the reader, «...al sedentario lector que prefiera Castilla la Vieja desde su butaca al lado de la chimenea...» [4] He is quick to confess that he cannot hope to write a definitive work on the subject. The region cannot be thoroughly savored with one «gulp».

> Pero querer llegar hasta el final de todo, querer apurar de un sorbo el vaso inmenso de Castilla la Vieja, sería empresa con la que el vagabundo, que procura ser un vagabundo honesto, no podría cargar sobre sus hombros. [5]

Yet, in the formal expression of modesty, his assertion that he cannot hope to exhaust the topic of «Castilla la Vieja» suggests neither has anyone else. At least, he proposes to search for the soul of the region with humility and self-sacrificing objectivity.

> El vagabundo..., no cree que estas páginas puedan comenzarse bajo otro signo que el de la humilde paciencia, bajo otra

---

[2] Camilo José Cela, *Judíos, Moros y Cristianos*, Ediciones Destino, Barcelona, 1956, p. 15.
[3] *Ibid.*, p. 14.
[4] *Ibid.*, p. 14.
[5] *Ibid.*, p. 15.

estrella que la de más limpia sencillez y la más deliberada y sangrante renunciación.[6]

The unique literary aspect of this book rests on the blend of factual account and the creation of artistic experiences, effectively intertwined in the narration so as to form one symphonic theme: the livingness of «Castilla la Vieja». Even the dreary and somnolent facts of history, carefully and accurately described by the author, come alive with the intensity of the moment.

The pauses of the archaelogical narrations are filled with the day to day triviliaties of the author and his characters. But creative fiction does not detract from the historical analysis; on the contrary, the reader is given time to digest the past as he encounters the relief of the present. Moreover, the author employs contemporaneity to verify or disprove the archives of time. And thus, he proceeds to count walls or steps or roads in order that he may compare results with the credulous assumptions of more lethargic researchers.

In the best tradition of Spanish scholarship, as lexicographers had done fifty years earlier, Cela undertakes to examine personally the remaining archaeological data of history. His intense desire to experience the totality of Spain, his need to penetrate the inner meaning of Hispanic values, is now translated into creative scholarship. He cannot accept the dubious truth of other investigators, who indolently relied on the truth of their ancestors; he must search for himself; he must feel the vestiges of the past with his own senses. The project is not motivated wholly by a labor of pleasurable love, but rather by a sense of responsibility toward the understanding of Spain. Fundamentally, Cela's only labor of love is the love of life. He would rather witness the feminine antics of a pretty girl than the charm of a cathedral. «El vagabundo prefiere una muchacha peinándose la mata de pelo ante un espejillo de seis reales a la puerta de un chozo de adobes, a una catedral gótica o a un jardín al estilo francés.»[7]

The lyrical aspect of Cela's search for historical truth furnishes a dramatic theme for *Judíos, Moros y Cristianos*. Cela is intent on establishing himself as a scholar. By means of irony, his most eficacious weapon, he shatters the mirror of absoluteness that historical

---

[6] *Ibid.*, p. 16.
[7] *Ibid.*, p. 22.

research purports to reflect. And upon the broken pieces, he builds for himself a new temple of wisdom. His first task, then, is to express the inadequacy of the old order of knowledge regarding «Castilla la Vieja». «Este pico de Peñalara lo sitúa el Instituto Geográfico a 2.430 metros sobre el nivel del mar, la guía de carreteras a 2.649, el Espasa a 2.406 y el atlas de Stieler a 2.405. El vagabundo piensa que lo más probable es que ande entre los 2.000 y los 3.000.» [8] Once he has established the disorder in facts, he undertakes to ridicule the generic scholar, «un maestro de escuela, la mar de culto». Don Mamerto de la Alameda, the school master, is a supercilious individual who thrives on the ignorance of others. «A don Mamerto de la Alameda le daba mucha risa que el vagabundo no entendiera nada de peces.» [9] The poor pedant, lacking in imagination, appears stunned when the vagabond discerns the obvious answers.

>—¿Y el *Barbus bocagei?*
>—Hombre, eso yo creo que es el barbo, ¿no?
>—Sí, señor, acertó usted. ¿Y el *Salmo fario?*
>—¿Cómo?
>—El *Salmo fario.*
>—Pues..., ¿el salmón?
>—Sí, señor, ha vuelto a acertar usted.
>—Vaya, me alegro. [10]

Further on, in a more serious mood, Cela criticizes the linguists of the Academy Dictionary for their naive assumptions about the language spoken in Segovia.

> ...estos castellanos de Segovia no hablan el castellano, cosa que le cuesta trabajo creer, o los académicos del diccionario no se han echado al campo con un cuaderno para apuntar lo que en el diccionario no viene apuntado... [11]

---

[8] *Ibid.*, p. 18. Subsequently, the point is made time and again. For example, «Entre los eruditos hay opiniones para todos los gustos; así es mejor porque cada cual escoge la que más le agrada, como en los bazares.» «En algunos libros, no dice que doña Velasquita y doña Elvira fueran hermanas; en otros, sí.» «Algunos dicen que el acueducto es obra de los egipcios, otros piensan que lo levantaron los romanos y aún otros, en fin, hablan de si no sería el diablo el arquitecto.» *Ibid.*, pp. 108, 109, and 132.
[9] *Ibid.*, p. 23.
[10] *Ibid.*, p. 23.
[11] *Ibid.*, p. 36.

He then proceeds to make up his own brief dictionary on the regionalisms of Segovia. He too can rise to the lofty level of lexicography. However, not wishing to appear so presumptuous as don Mamerto de la Alameda, he reverts to humor and states that had he only alphabetized his dictionary, he too would have become a philologist.

> El vagabundo, después de leer y releer su lista, piensa que, si la hubiera puesto por el orden del abecé, a estas horas podría andar por la calle mirando de costadillo como un filólogo. En fin, ¡otra vez será! [12]

In reality, Cela is quite serious about his erudition. Frequently, he resorts to humor in order to conceal his own inner conflicts, his frustrations.

In the composition of his previous wanderings, Cela sought to palpate his land solely as an artist. In *Judíos, Moros y Cristianos*, the vagabond's main purpose is to rediscover historical truth. To be sure, the author does not divest himself of his creativity, but here the artistry, the recreation of life, becomes the stage for the drama of history. The trivialities of the present constitute the refrain for the song of the past. Thus, Cela recalls the events of other centuries, while he listens to the tales of the inhabitants he meets.

> Ayllón es pueblecito grande, ruinoso e historiado. En Ayllón hubo una parroquia de Santa María de la Media Vida. En Ayllón, el condestable Luna, cuando perdía, se retiraba a reponer sus fuerzas y sus armas. En Ayllón, el conde de Miranda cobraba las alcabalas, las martiniegas y las tercias reales...
>
> En Ayllón predicó San Vicente Ferrer, que era racista, y que consiguió del rey que obligase a los moros a usar capuces verdes con lunas claras, y a los judíos a llevar una marca sangrienta en el tabardo. [13]

It is as though he felt inhibited about «spouting» history. In the beginning, he is quite shy about fulfilling the role of historian. Having ridiculed scholars, Cela is sensitive about becoming one of his own caricatures.

---

[12] *Ibid.*, pp. 37-38.
[13] *Ibid.*, p. 42.

As the narration progresses, Cela becomes less diffident, but the change is not abrupt. At first he employs the literary «trick» of having another character in the role of historian. It is the old mendicant who carefully, amidst the deliberate interruptions of the author, narrates the detailed account of Roa's past. Embarrassed by the display of knowledge, Cela not only punctuates the narration with personal digressions but in addition feigns to be amused by the memory of the old man.

> El vagabundo empieza a pensar que su amigo, del que aun no sabe el nombre, debe ser un sabio en penitencia o un bachiller al que la historia y los latines sorbieron la sesera.
> —¡Buena memoria tiene usted!
> —Sí, señor, cierto es que tengo buena memoria. Y clara inteligencia, feliz palabra y largas horas de estudio.
> —Sí, sí...
> El mendigo se había definido con una seriedad profunda. [14]

Again, Cela is quite serious, and really very proud of his command of facts.

Since Cela cannot cease to be Cela, the artist, his view of life or history is novelistic. As the man of flesh and blood, or in the role of Scholar, Cela is inventive. In his vision of the past as well as in his experience of the present, Cela moves, from the sphere of appearance to the probing of inner existence. Not content with merely creating an external figure who will act as his prolocutor in matters of archaeological data, the author gives his character a life of his own. The existence of the narrator is built upon the literary tradition of the *escudero* of *Lazarillo de Tormes*. But here the «type» is personalized. It is given a consciousness of its role. And so, we have a person who is aware of his being a «misfit» in the society of present day Spain. First of all, the man is an anarchist. «No, hijo, que yo no mando ni obedezco.» [15] Proud of being a «don», his title is his one illusion. Once he discovers that the vagabond cannot be too sure of having a similar title himself, the mendicant regally begs that he be permitted not to address the author formally.

---

[14] *Ibid.*, p. 67.
[15] *Ibid.*, p. 70.

> ...¿Usted tiene el don?
> —No, señor, mejor dicho, no lo sé bien. Antes, cuando me escribían alguna carta, me lo ponían
> —¿Pero no está seguro de tenerlo?
> —No, señor, seguro no estoy.
> —Entonces me permitirá usted que no le dé tratamiento. [16]

The irony here is somewhat lyrical, and it serves a didactic purpose. We know, of course, that Cela by virtue of being considered for membership in the Royal Academy could look forward to the right to such a title, and even to *excelentísimo*. [17] Yet, it cannot be said that the author's self-adulation is the mendicant's only reason for being. Long after we have forgotten the minuscule facts about Roa, we remember the man who does not deign to work.

> ...Yo no tengo oficio porque no quise y también porque no pude querer tenerlo. Como usted sabe, en Castilla los hidalgos no tenemos oficio, aunque con los revueltos tiempos que corren, también nos hayamos quedado sin beneficio. El trabajo es una maldición de Dios y el que trabaja, si no lo hace con resignación y para ofrecérselo a Él, peca gravemente, amén de que pierde la nobleza. [18]

This *hidalgo* is not a mere pretext, nor an object of ridicule. On the contrary, in his expression of pride he appears as a lofty reminder of history. It is his person that recalls the grandeur of Spain, and the author expresses this idea with profound sympathy and admiration. And thus, the beggar is elevated from the gravel that surrounds him to the loftiness of the sky.

> Sentado sobre un montón de grava del camino, don Toribio de Mogrovejo de Ortiz de la Seca y de Castilmimbre de Fuentespreadas y de López de Valdeavellano, se despiojaba paciente, antiguo y orgulloso, igual que el gavilán. [19]

Although Cela impulsively continues to create characters and situations as he travels, eventually he acquires enough self-poise to assume,

---

[16] *Ibid.*, pp. 70-71.
[17] The actual date on which he became an «Académico» was February 21, 1957. Of course, by the time this book appeared, the definite possibility of election to the *Real Academia Española* already existed.
[18] *Ibid.*, p. 71.
[19] *Ibid.*, p. 71.

himself, the role of historian. Without intermediaries, he displays phenomenal erudition in the humanistic fields that mold the study of history. The odyssey of Cela recalls the state of mind of Don Quijote who in part I of his adventures retains a consciousness of trying to be a knight errant while still being Don Alonso Quijano. So it is with Cela. While in the regions of Segovia, he maintains a self-consciousness about his position as a scholar; he needs to speak indirectly. By the time he reaches Ávila, however, he is as Don Quijote in part II; he has the assurance of having realized his dream. If Don Quijote and Sancho become convinced of their achievements by a reading of their own exploits, Cela too must have felt reassured about his new identity by rereading his description of Segovia. Actually *Judíos, Moros y Cristianos,* composed in a span of several years and distinct sojourns, could be considered to have two parts, Segovia and Ávila. [20]

In Ávila Cela speaks with the confidence of an oracle. He approaches the environs of the great city in a car; he comes now as an aristocrat. «El vagabundo adoptó un aire interesante. —Es que desde Cuéllar, ¿sabe usted?, me trajeron unos amigos en su automóvil...» [21] But whatever air he assumes, he must first palpate life around him.

> Un can de negras lanas y cara de fraile, hoza, igual que un jabalí, en un montoncito de basura. Desde un balcón de pobre y misteriosa traza, un niño se cisca sobre el mundo, con un infinito y desentendido gesto de desprecio. Las campanas de las iglesias y de los conventos llaman, con su dolida, con su quejumbrosa voz, a su clientela de beatas. Un mozo arrea una tunda regular a una mula exquelética y desvencijada, llena de blanquecinas mataduras en carne viva. Una niña modosita y amarga, una niña que cree que es pecado sentir que el breve seno se le despierta, cruza con un albo y blando paquete bajo el brazo... [22]

The next step is to recall history to himself in a stream of consciousness as he half-heartedly listens to the interrogations of the inhabitants, who are curious about the appearance of the learned vagabond. Finally,

---

[20] There is in print a separate paperback edition on Ávila, a sort of guide, written by Cela. It is a «dehumanized» or «objectivized» version of Cela's travels in this region. It would be useful for the tourist.
[21] *Ibid.,* p. 165.
[22] *Ibid.,* pp. 165-166.

in form of direct soliloquy he faces his readers and speaks out with conviction and determination. Now he is prepared to pontificate.

> ...Las murallas de Ávila, que pintan un rectángulo bastante regular y limpio, tienen media legua de rodeo y presentan, a lo largo de él, noventa torres, y no ochenta y ocho, como en todas partes se dice. El error, según piensa el vagabundo, viene del manuscrito que exhumó don José María Quadrado, detrás de quien parecen haber ido todos: Azorín, el penúltimo. [23]

As Cela becomes established in the «chair of history», his preoccupation with documentation wanes. He relaxes his grip on facts, and permits himself the luxury of being subjective. Having proved himself an «original» scholar, he reverts to his natural state, that of being a passionate recreator of Spanish life. For all his undisputed knowledge of history, Cela appears more comfortable in his role as a creative writer. It is when he writes as a «lover» of Spain that characters and situations come alive. As an historian, he imparts novel facts; as a novelist he perpetuates the human existence of his surroundings.

Cela had already proved himself a «lover» of Spain in the previous book of travels, *Del Miño al Bidasoa*. But the affection was somewhat materialistic. It was based in some part on the fertility of the land and the industriousness of the people. The vision of productivity filled the author with a feeling of satiation that he had not known before in his itenerant palpation of Spanish life. In brief, Cela was overcome with a feeling of copiousness. The mere absence of hunger was a source of joy for him.

In *Judíos, Moros y Cristianos* (the word order of the title is deliberate, indeed), [24] Cela declares himself a romantic lover of Spain, as one who loves the sins as well as the virtues of his beloved. The grief that he experiences upon witnessing the wretchedness of his compatriots

---

[23] In a letter to me dated March 26, 1962, Cela explains his ironical intent. I had thought that he had someone in mind as *último*. «...Cuando dije que Azorín fue el *penúltimo* que cayó en el error de suponer que las torres de la muralla de Ávila eran ochenta y ocho y no noventa —como son en realidad— hablé en sentido figurado y le llamé el *penúltimo* porque pensé que algún otro habría caído después en idéntico error.»

[24] It would certainly appear that Cela's intention was not merely to shock his readers, a position not uncommon to him, but also to express a descending scale of historical values.

intensifies his feeling of oneness with his people. For the vagabond «que ama a España sobre todas las cosas», [25] the dreariest vision of life evokes sympathy.

> San Vicente de Arévalo es pueblo pobre, como todos estos por los que el vagabundo anda y—por ahora— andará, y *sin más que ver que lo que quiera mirarse con amor*. Pueblos sin carretera, sin ferrocarril, sin más agua que la que Dios manda y la tierra quiere devolver; pueblos sobrios y ahorcados a la fuerza; pueblos místicos y heroicos, en mejores tiempos, y hoy agazapados en el barbecho, igual que conejos temerosos; pueblos a los que bate el lobo, y el rayo, y la sequía; pueblos que han olvidado el color de la hartura y que siguen ignorando el de la felicidad. [26]

In the early works of Cela, love expressed itself in the form of tears and blood. Blood, in particular, was the symbol of his living experience, that force which joined him to his people. But now he suffers no more in his integration with the land. His love lacks the agonizing fire of youth. It is now the fulfilment of life. He need not crave imaginary pleasures that do not exist; he can be happy even in the wretchedness that is Spain.

> El vagabundo..., se siente dichoso y acompañado, sin escuchar más ruidos que los ruidos del mundo—un asno que rebuzna, una gallina que ha puesto un huevo, un niño que llora infinitamente, una paloma que zurea, un látigo que restalla, un gañán que canta—ni aspirar más aromas que los hondos aromas del mundo—el del pan que se cuece, el del aire de la mañana, el del manso y cálido estiércol, el de la flor que brota en los terrones, el de la moza que desrabera la parva del trigo cascalbo, el del agua que brilla en el rezumadero. [27]

Cela seems to be possessed of that consciousness of life that sustains his literary persons even when life appears to be without meaning, without direction. He can see himself as an author sees his character. He is well aware of the change that has taken place within the land and more important still, within himself. Thus, he recalls his early

---

[25] *Ibid.*, p. 236.
[26] *Ibid.*, p. 182 (the italics are mine).
[27] *Ibid.*, pp. 182-183.

vision of Spain as expressed in *Viaje a la Alcarria*, when people were in a stupor, living without memory and consequently without names. They were nourished only by a vague recollection of the past.

> ...En España—viejo país—cada rincón tiene su nombre, no hay más que buscarlo. Por la Alcarria, en otro de sus viajes, el vagabundo se topó, más allá de las Tetas de Viana, por Viana y por la Puerta, con un regato sin nombre, con un riatillo hospiciano y sin papeles que daba pena verlo. La gente, que había perdido la memoria de cómo se llamaba, le decía, incluso con ternura, el arroyo.[28]

The hymn of *Judíos, Moros y Cristianos* might be entitled «Spain for better or for worse». And so Cela calls his last chapter of the book, «Donde, Mejor O Peor, Se Fundó España». No one, says the author, can be certain that Spain would be better off if it were not as it is. «Sin el duro cabildeo de los toros de Guisando, España no hubiera sido España y otra cosa—nadie debe atreverse a jurar si mejor o peor—viviría hoy en nuestra parcela.»[29] The «bitter» image of Spain is symbolized by the forlorn bulls of Guisando. «Vivos de milagro»,[30] the bulls' existence defies reason. Their way of life may be agonizing but they, themselves, inspire admiration. In their case, to have continued their existence is in itself an accomplishment.

The composition of *Judíos, Moros y Cristianos* does not follow a unilateral plane of unabashed admiration for all that is Spanish. As a thinker, as an analyst of Hispanic values, Cela reaches some personal conclusions. And unquestionably, his personal position permeates his process of creativity. However, in the forging of characters and situations Cela maintains his complex vision of life; he continues to express simultaneously a perspective of opposites. Thus, we have creative circumstances as well as moments of history that are depicted with a sense of irony which combines the ridiculous and the sublime. To be sure, love is the motivating force at all times, but for Cela love is not only that force which creates but also that force which destroys.[31]

---

[28] *Ibid.*, pp. 263-264.
[29] *Ibid.*, p. 301.
[30] *Ibid.*, p. 301.
[31] In February of '61 while translating part of my manuscript into Spanish for Cela in the haven of Palma de Mallorca, I recall how Cela jus-

In his creative process, harmony is but one possible expression of love. More frequently, an image of grotesqueness will express his profound sympathy for humanity, for Cela is more affected by life's sense of disproportion than by the symmetry that for him scarcely exists.

The pathetic but hilarious account of the beautiful girl who was cursed by uncontrollable flatus, a story which would hardly fit in any other historical account of Spain, reveals Cela's propensity for the absurd. The reader may hate himself for it, but he cannot help finding it amusing. That is to say, the fantastic crude tale, as told by the quack who extracts Cela's tooth for two *pesetas*, acquires literary reality. This is made patent by the author's refusal to visit Fuentesaúco, the scene of the grotesque event. Cela feels honor bound to respect the exile of his primitive healer, don Fabián, whose leeches were overwhelmed by the disease of the beautiful girl.

Cela recognizes no sacred symbols. Even the factual and legendary accounts of Spanish history, held in high esteem by the inhabitants of Segovia and Ávila, are seen in the light of absurdity. Cela's love is distinguished by irreverence rather than by submission. He delights in being iconoclastic; in effect, he cannot remain otherwise, for long. His intuitive novelistic perspective adds a dimension of profanity to all that is holy. The process of humanizing myths is not altogether frivolous; often it contains a sad lament, a strident cry. Such is the case with the «Virgin of the Cows» who makes her appearance in «la mitología cristiana»[32] by permitting the animals to plow the land while their master attends Mass. The event does not surprise Cela who is sensitive to the Spaniard's aversion for work. «Al vagabundo nada le sorprende que pase esto en un país donde las únicas gentes que mostraron algo de afición a trabajar, tampoco mucha, fueron los judíos y los moriscos.»[33] Similarly, in describing the church of San Vicente, which represents the miracle of conversion, the author suggests that a serpent would be frightening enough to make a Christian of anyone. «La serpiente, al verlo, se le enroscó alrededor del cuerpo y el judío, quizás del susto, se hizo cristiano...»[34]

---

tified this position. He insisted that Vicente Aleixandre had intuitively expressed that position by the title *La destrucción o el amor*.

[32] *Ibid.*, p. 198.
[33] *Ibid.*, p. 199.
[34] *Ibid.*, p. 208.

The piercing humor of Cela touches upon all aspects of existence, human and divine. There are many Virgins in Spain, and the author takes pleasure in telling about all of them. In Spain, even the adulteresses have their patron.

> La Virgen de la Chilla, en cierto modo, podría entenderse como la patrona de las malmaridadas; hay algunos que, a la malmaridada, se conforman con decirle casada infiel. [35]

And the merchants display on their wall their crude prayers asking their Saint to spare them of debtors.

> Santo Ángel de la Guarda
> que libras a los pecadores,
> líbranos a nosotros
> de los malos pagadores. [36]

These verses «cargados de moscas» represent the nadiral level of piety. Even the author pretends to be offended by such profanity. Indeed, in *Judíos, Moros y Cristianos* religion has many faces.

Cela's intent to recreate life in Segovia and Ávila reaches such missionary proportions that he even resorts to statistics, charts and drawings in order to convey his experiences. Ávila, in particular, becomes the object of his homage. Here the numerous signs denote the dissimilar degrees of charity. In some instances, the presumed expressions of brotherly love are quite commercial; they announce a meal in exchange for labor. But if there is no sense of charitable harmony among his Catholic brethren, the few Protestants he meets are equally lacking in logic. Their congregation convenes to read the Bible; more than half are illiterate. [37]

Cela rejoices in the disproportion of life. Lofty concepts or trivial expressions of human existence are seen in conflict. There is no harmony between their inner and outer reality. Be they facts or be they myths, the author thrives on their inconsistencies. The lands of Sego-

---

[35] *Ibid.*, p. 270.
[36] *Ibid.*, p. 210.
[37] «En Guisando también hay cristianos protestantes que, a falta de capilla se reúnen en casa del Colás, a leer la Biblia. Más de la mitad, bastante más de la mitad de la población de Guisando, no sabe leer ni escribir.» *Ibid.*, p. 274.

via and Ávila are the most purely Castilian regions. They represent the heart and spirit of Christian Spain. Yet, it is here that we find living vestiges of Moorish life.

> Casavieja es pueblo tímido y pobre, con el nombre bien puesto... En Casavieja es la invitada, cuando la hay, quien sirve, antes que a nadie y en señal de respeto, al dueño de la casa; los árabes debieron dejar su semilla, por aquí. [38]

Naturally, the custom obtains meaning when there are guests. The town is not known for its abundant supply of food.

Hunger is never treated lightly in the world of Cela. It is a grim reality. Although he, himself, as a member of the upper class and a one-time defender of the caste system [39] has been spared the plague of starvation, he has felt as his own curse the hunger of his people. It may be that his preferential condition has filled him with sensations of guilt. Possibly, his compulsion to travel as a vagabond is but a form of self-punishment, a sort of masochistic obssession, because Cela, the man of flesh and blood, loves the luxuries of life. The artistic personality of Cela, however, cries out for food. He views as casuistry the orthodox position that the meek will inherit the earth. The promise of eternal salvation lacks the virtue of earthly abundance. And this, in opposition to his favorite Saint, San Juan de la Cruz! [40] The rebellious spirit of hunger recognizes no idols.

> San Juan de la Cruz cantó a la pobreza como una bendición de Dios. Al vagabundo le aturde y le sobrecoge la pobreza del padre de familia que no sabe ni puede, aunque bien quisiera, llenar la panza de los suyos treinta días al mes. No hay miseria más honda que el hambre que se reparte. [41]

On the subject of religion, when the teachings of the Church do not become a mask for penury, Cela can be quite humorous. He derives

---

[38] *Ibid.*, p. 294.

[39] During the Spanish Civil War he fought as a corporal in Franco's army. Although not born into aristocracy, his family has enjoyed some position and above all, the security of «bread».

[40] Cela has written a delightful book for children on the life of San Juan de la Cruz. For Cela, children constitute his most delicate audience. See bibl'ography.

[41] *Ibid.*, p. 282.

great satisfaction in questioning the purity of Christianity. Already, in order to irritate the Franco regime, he had jocosely alluded to himself as an impure Aryan.[42] Here he tells about a relative of his, a martyr with a heretical name.

> El vagabundo tuvo un pariente de esta religión, mártir en Damasco, que llegó a beato... El pariente del vagabundo tenía nombre de hereje; se llamaba Juan Jacobo.[43]

The observation has an air of sympathetic frivolity. The critic is one who finds it more difficult not to believe than to believe in myths.[44] In the last analysis, thaumaturgy holds a greater fascination than logic for Cela.

The author, himself, does not escape ridicule. He mocks himself as he mocks others. Even his Don Juanesque accomplishments, an area which might be deemed sensitive to the masculine ego, meet the fate of other myths. The success of his romantic venture rests on his likeness to a dead husband. «Al vagabundo..., una dama enlutada le cobró afición. Al vagabundo, en ocasiones, se le transparenta un misterioso airecillo de marido muerto.»[45] Following the interlude, as if to accentuate the absurdity of his conquest, the author is reminded of his resemblance to the deceased husband. Moreover, the levity ascribed to the woman detracts further from his achievement. The one immutable aspect is the undisputed beauty of the lady. Thus, his sense of aesthetics redeems him and saves him from appearing as a completely undiscerning ghost.

> —¿De Bohoyo? En Bohoyo tenía yo un sobrino que se parecía a usted, en los andares... Al pobre lo mató una

---

[42] «Mis completos nombres de pila son los siguientes: ...; Santiago, por haber nacido a la sombra de la peña donde apareció el cadáver del Apóstol, y Abraham, Zacarías y Leví, probablemente, porque no soy ario puro del todo.» *Baraja de Invenciones*, see «Breve Autobiografía del Inventor». The Jewish name is fictitious. Cela's intention was to puncture the racial myth of Hitler, Franco's benefactor during the Civil War.

[43] *Judíos, Moros y Cristianos*, p. 282.

[44] «El vagabundo, que más bien cree que deja de creer en brujas y en milagros, en tradiciones, en leyendas y en aparecidos, se siente feliz—y también ligeramente preocupado—en estos escenarios castellanos y confusos, oscuros, casi siempre, y a veces deslumbradores y taumatúrgicos.» *Ibid.*, p. 129.

[45] *Ibid.*, p. 259.

chispa, va ya para un año... No sé lo que se habrá hecho de la viuda... A lo mejor, se casó otra vez... Ya sabe usted lo que son las mujeres de hoy en día... Era una guapa moza, ésa es la verdad...»[46]

If Cela scoffs at the image of himself as a lover, he indulges in panegyrics regarding Cela, the writer. As a literary critic, he is quick to recognize his own originality. «El vagabundo, que en ningún libro encontró..., arbitró el fabricarse, sobre el camino, una geografía para su uso.»[47] The theatre of Calderón de la Barca, on the other hand, does not make a favorable impression on him because it lacks poetic truth.[48] His evaluation of Lorca is in itself poetic. He does not attempt to rationalize style.[49] On literary generalities, he finds that poetry is not consonant with civilization. The latter not only seems to kill germs, but also poetic genius. «A más civilización, menos tirar papeles al suelo y menos atar latas al rabo de los gatos, pero también menos poesía.»[50]

Early in the book Cela had declared himself a lover of the unharmonious. In fact, he rehearsed speaking to himself so as to assure the fulfilment of discord. «El vagabundo, a veces, se divierte hablando a solas para ensayarse en el complicado arte de no llegar a un acuerdo jamás.»[51] For the author, the promise of order represents the fraud perpetrated by the regime that emerged victorious after the Spanish Civil War. At one time in his life, as he fought along the triumphant forces of Franco, Cela must have exalted the concept of order; he must have passionately believed in the attainment of harmony. Now he reacts with hostility and fear toward the memory of that war, in which human life was molded in the image of blood. Cela, who appears impervious to crudity, cruelty, and the lowest forms of

---

[46] *Ibid.*, p. 268.
[47] *Ibid.*, p. 220.
[48] «En todo caso, al vagabundo le sucede, con las catedrales, lo que con el teatro de don Pedro Calderón de la Barca, que nunca acaba de parecerle verdad del todo.» *Ibid.*, p. 206.
[49] «Al vagabundo le parece que la expresión 'mugieron como dos siglos' la usó el poeta en todos sus poéticos alcances y como imagen de furia y desesperación, de abatimiento, de dolor y de desolación. Lorca, al entender del vagabundo, dijo 'dos siglos' poéticamente, como poéticamente pudo haber dicho 'mil siglos'.» *Ibid.*, p. 305.
[50] *Ibid.*, p. 276.
[51] *Ibid.*, p. 52.

debauchery, can not withstand the recollection of the devastation of which he was a part. He can listen to fanciful and ferocious narrations of events, but he does not wish to be reminded of the Civil War.

> —¡El fuego de Briongos, en el campo de Burgos!... —¡El fuego de Cabrejas del Pinar, en la tierra de Soria!... —¡El fuego... El vagabundo le interrumpió. —No siga! [52]

Naturally, the theme cannot be ignored entirely, especially in a book dedicated to the rectification of specious information. The sanctity of historical truth must be preserved. Besides, he needs to flay himself. It is his manner of atonement.

Judíos, Moros y Cristianos, the exterior title of this book, represents a new battle cry in the career of Camilo José Cela. It has for him the force that «Santiago» had for Castilians during the *Reconquista*. [53] It needs no elaboration, certainly no rational justification. It is a creed, a new religion of passionate thought, an existential revelation. Except for some minor allusions to a Semitic heritage, Cela does not strive to essentialize his imposing title. Belief is sufficient unto itself. In the new perspective of the author, Christian Spain is but an outer image of a land which is irreducibly composed of three distinct cultures, Christian, Jewish and Moorish. There is, of course, a sense of ironic justice in bestowing the title of *Judíos, Moros y Cristianos* on «Castilla la vieja», the spiritual heart of Spain.

Whether Cela became a standard-bearer of Américo Castro's concept of Spanish history because of conviction or because it gave him another opportunity to rebel against tradition as embodied in the regime of General Franco, is a question that may have to be answered by two yeses. There are no absolutes in the life of Cela. Obviously, Cela must have been in a state of receptiveness when Castro's interpretation of history was revealed to him. In a sense, he reacted to the «incitement» as a novelistic hero. And his proselytism encouraged his vengeance. [54]

---

[52] *Ibid.*, p. 122.
[53] See Castro's *España en su historia*, Capítulo IV, «Cristianismo frente a Islam, La creencia en Santiago de Galicia».
[54] «Escribir es mi gran venganza» clamors Cela. *Papeles de Son Armadans*, Año II, Tomo VI, Núm. XVII, August, 1957.

More significant than the conjectural question of personal motivation is the matter of artistic intent—and the degree of its fulfilment. The salient achievement of Cela in *Judíos, Moros y Cristianos* is that without sacrificing artistic creation, without abdicating his position as the master of disproportion, he succeeds in proving himself an able and original historical scholar. In his ironical manner, Cela had made it clear in the beginning that he would strive not to appear ostentatious about his erudition because historians too had to eat while he already was making a living as a writer. «El vagabundo también sabe sus cosas, aunque procure disimularlas por aquello de que todo el mundo tiene que comer, incluso los historiadores y los eruditos, y él, a su manera, ya se las va arreglando.» [55] Inevitably, the subsequent exhibition of knowledge is grandiloquent. And what is most offensive about it is that the content is irrefutable. Historians may forgive Cela's presentation of history as a living experience, but not his wealth of information and above all, not his original documented discoveries.

---

[55] *Op. Cit.*, p. 14.

XIII. PRIMER VIAJE ANDALUZ

Cela's last book of travels published up to date, *Primer Viaje Andaluz* (1959) represents the fruits of a labor of duty, rather than a labor of love. Having established himself as an erudite connoisseur of Hispanic life, Cela must include in his repertoire that significant segment of Spanish land known as *Andalucía*. In this region Cela is a stranger. «El sur, para el vagabundo, hombre del norte, es la remota e indescifrable tierra del piripao.» [1] He pursues his study of the towns and villages with a certain aloofness. In spite of several literary personal involvements, the author moves about his travels as a touristic vagabond, as one who is conscious of not belonging to the land he visits. For all its picturesqueness, *Andalucía* is but a vague interlude, virtually a superficial one, for the austere *gallego*, who can not feel at home in the frivolous atmosphere of Southern Spain.

The title, *Primer Viaje Andaluz,* implies an apology. Cela seems to be suggesting that his peregrination has not been fulfilled, that, at least, another trip need be made. Actually, it is highly doubtful that Cela will again explore the region which is so alien to him. The fact is that he has had to borrow from the experiences of earlier travels in order to give *Primer Viaje Andaluz* a semblance of reality. Were it not for the recurrence of familiar events and the reappearance of characters already known to us, the book might be lacking in literary substance. In that case, *Primer Viaje Andaluz* would have the appearance of a book of travel composed in the armchair of a comfortable study.

In terms of geographical coverage, and in spirit, *Primer Viaje Andaluz* has been Cela's fastest trip. He has not paused to savor the

---

[1] Camilo José Cela, *Primer Viaje Andaluz*, Editorial Noguer, S. A., Barcelona, 1959, p. 78.

land of *Andalucía* with the same fervor that he has «drunk» of Northern Spain. And even in reciting the history of this region, filled with colorful vestiges of Moorish civilization, the author's accounts lack the fire of life. Somehow or other, the narration remains in the past. Perhaps Cela's role as an historian has been too well played? From a scholarly point of view, the narration of the past is above reproach. It is accurate and honorable. He even displays some modesty regarding the knowledge he lacks. And this in a note, too! [2]

Primer Viaje Andaluz begins with the usual introductory remarks. But here the words constitute a rationalization for the «why» of travels. Cela feels the need to justify his present voyage. He seems unable to thrust himself into the Southern region of Spain with abandonment. He must retrace his final steps in *Del Miño al Bidasoa*, and base the start of his Andalusian venture on his farewell to Dupont. *Primer Viaje Andaluz* is but an epilogue to his travels. Cela feels tired; he is well aware that this may be his last vagabondage. «Pero el vagabundo—vuelve a pedir clemencia—está cansado; quizás, incluso, muy cansado y a lo mejor, el día que menos se piensa, pone punto final y definitivo al capítulo, ya extenso en lo que cabe, de sus vagabundajes.» [3] As it is, he does not immediately delve into the Andalusian scene. First, before entering the strange land, he wishes to explore «lovingly» that part of Spain that extends from the last pages of *Del Miño al Bidosoa* to the entrance of *Andalucía*. [4]

Cela is reluctant to visit Andalusia. He needs encouragment, and only an angel can persuade him «to go South». At that, the divine messenger must repeat the process of forceful revelation before it has an effect on the author. First it is the angel who speaks, then the bird who swallowed the ethereal figure intones the command. [5] The

---

[2] «*Fallah,* en árabe, significa huertano; el vagabundo cree que mencus no es voz de lengua mora y, en todo caso, no sabe lo que quiere decir. El poeta Mohammad Sabbag, amigo del vagabundo, tampoco lo sabía.» *Ibid.,* p. 315.

[3] *Ibid.,* p. 322.

[4] «Desde Narvarte hasta Despeñaperros hay más de media España, como se dijo. Y a esta media y más que media larga España, el vagabundo, en trance de caminarla otra vez, no quisiera dejar de mirarla, si brevemente, también amorosamente, antes de asomarse al extraño y dilatado confín andaluz.» *Ibid.,* p. 22.

[5] «—Al sur... Pero, ¿al sur? —Sí, al sur... —¿Al sur?... Sí, al sur...» *Ibid.,* pp. 77-78.

eventual undertaking is viewed as a sacrifice. Cela calls this chapter, the one in which the apparition takes place, «Decisión Casi Heroica y Rumbo al Sur».

Madrid, which presents a vision of horror,[6] is the real point of departure for the journey to Andalusia. In a truck, a novel form of travel for him, Cela is carried to his destination. In a manner of speaking, he has become a passive traveller. Only the piercing question regarding his role in the Civil War arouses his ire.

    —¿Usted con quién hizo la guerra?
    —¿Y a usted qué le importa?
    —Nada, usted perdone.[7]

He does not wish to be reminded of the War, and more particularly of his former faith in the Generalissimo. Moreover, Cela is intent on clarifying his artistic position: he does not write as a partisan. His love for Spain, his painful experience of life around him, transcends political affiliation. Cela is beyond the point of believing in circumscribed earthly salvation, if indeed he believes in any other.

The approach to Andalusia is a hasty one for Cela who «corre como un loco por el camino.»[8] He knows that he sins by coming into the region perched on a truck.[9] In the tradition of ambulatory knight-errantry only on his feet should he have relied for support. «A veces el vagabundo discurre que los pies tienen alma, como alma tiene el corazón. En el camino, son los pies los que piensan; también los que aman y los que padecen.»[10] But apparently, Cela is no longer a true vagabond. If erudition has impaired his genius, comfort has spoiled his primitive delights. Palma de Mallorca beckons!

Primer Viaje Andaluz reflects rather clearly the personal circumstances of the author. He often makes no attempt to mask himself in

---

    [6] Madrid is still the symbol of depravity. «Hacia el arrabal, los ojos del vagabundo contemplan un tentador y venenoso paisaje de casuchas ruines y mulas cojas, de niños harapientos y niñas preñadas y precozmente greñudas, de tullidos que se rascan la sarna con un imperial y sacrosanto entusiasmo y de golfos que esquilman gilís con las arteras suertes de la carteta.» *Ibid.*, p. 83.
    [7] *Ibid.*, p. 86.
    [8] *Ibid.*, p. 93.
    [9] «Esto de trotar, sin más ni más y venga y venga, por el camino abajo y a lomos de un hierro trepidante y rugidor, es algo que al vagabundo se le antoja punto menos que un grave pecado.» *Ibid.*, p. 93.
    [10] *Ibid.*, p. 14.

literary garbs. Perhaps it is because Cela mistrusts the audience's comprehension of subtleties that he resorts to explicit directness. Perhaps he no longer needs to distinguish between himself as a man of flesh and blood and himself as a character in a book. At any rate, with unmistakable clarity he makes it known to us that his exile is voluntary, that it is he who chooses to disdain the peninsula, as he disdains the ruling class.

> Al vagabundo, de no ser que vive muy alejado del trajín de este valle de lágrimas y de sus pompas y vanidades (sépase que por propia voluntad y para mantener tranquila su conciencia), le hubiera gustado, más de una vez, preguntar a los conservadores españoles qué es lo que se proponen conservar. [11]

In a similar manner he relates to us his knowledge of Arabic [12] and his universal appreciation of feminine pulchritude. [13] Cela finds women beautiful wherever he goes. In this respect, the southern part of Spain is for him as interesting as any.

In this book the conservatives become the object of the author's scorn. Whereas the past can be mythologically beautiful, Cela reacts with hostility against those who would believe in the past as a way of life. As an historian, he recounts the merits of antiquity; as a man of the twentieth century, he seeks to live in accordance with the new possibilites. The conservatives, on the other hand, seek to «embalm time». [14] Consequently, nothing but the distortion of things past is preserved.

In his happier moments Cela reiterates his thankfulness for dreams [15] and above all his gladness for life. «Viva la vida» he

---

[11] *Ibid.*, p. 108.

[12] «En la iglesia de la Asunción de Nuestra Señora quedan los restos de los restos de dos lápidas árabes que aún se pueden leer por quien sepa los signos moros, que parecen lombricitas puestas en fila. Una dice, entre otras cosas...» *Ibid.*, p. 107.

[13] «El vagabundo, sin pronunciarse por ninguna, que todas le parecen adorables y dignas de loa y encomio...» *Ibid.*, p. 110.

[14] «...si sus inquilinos, en vez de empecinarse en la funeraria actitud de embalsamar el tiempo ido, eso que siempre acaba pudriéndose, porque es ley de vida, se hubieran esforzado, día a día y con aplicación, en conservar el presente...» *Ibid.*, p. 223.

[15] «El vagabundo es tan pobre que si vacía su arca con un vicio, ha de casarlo en sueños con el otro. Pero el vagabundo no se queja porque oyó contar—y prefirió creerlo—que hay quienes ni sueñan.» *Ibid.*, pp. 118-119.

exclaims.[16] Wherever Cela goes, whatever he does, he is happy to be alive. On another occasion he had said that if life was a struggle, death was no less of an agony.[17] In the company of gypsies as in the company of the elite, Cela offers his praise to life.

The literary aspects of *Primer Viaje Andaluz* rests on the creation of quaint characters who bestow upon Cela a dimension of fanciful existence. Through the reappearance of old friends from *Del Miño al Bidasoa* and *Viaje a la Alcarria* as well as through the invention of new figures, the pattern of artistic reality is woven. Especially, the well established fictionalized entities of the earlier works give meaning and form to the world of irreality that would be Cela and *Andalucía*. As if sensing the incompatibility that exists between himself and his milieu, Cela calls on the past for help.

The recollection of past travels and the reappearance of old characters not only serve to give form to the artistic fabric of *Primer Viaje Andaluz*, but in addition they accentuate the changes that have taken place in Spain since the nineteen forties. In Lora Cela meets «Martín el de las alpargatas», a fictionalized entity of long standing. «El vagabundo..., se encontró con un amigo del que nada sabía desde mucho tiempo atrás: desde que anduviera, allá por el mes de junio de 1946, por las honestas tierras de la Alcarria.»[18] But here Martín is prosperous. He has been mechanized, as it were, and now he travels in style. Cela cannot conceal his admiration for Martín's new acquisition and he succumbs to the temptation of paying homage to the motorcycle. «Al vagabundo, ...no le costó demasiado trabajo vencer sus propios escrúpulos y conciencias para acabar subiéndose en la moto.»[19] Thus, «Martín el de las alpargatas», now a successful businessman, becomes «Martín el de la moto». Nonetheless, Cela's vision of Spain has not been blurred by the apparent economic progress. He knows that the existence of wealth among some indicates the affliction of hunger among many more. «Linares es pueblo rico o, mejor dicho, pueblo donde, al lado del hambre, corre el dinero.»[20] And on the

---

[16] *Ibid.*, p. 209.
[17] «El vagabundo, que ha abandonado la lucha, sabe que la vida es lucha, pero que lo contrario de la vida, que es la muerte, es lucha también.» *Judíos, Moros y Cristianos*, p. 33.
[18] *Ibid.*, p. 241.
[19] *Ibid.*, p. 242.
[20] *Ibid.*, p. 131.

subject of starvation, he continues to be intransigent. «—Sí; de grandes cenas están las sepulturas llenas. Las que no se cuentan son las que se llenaron de resultas de acostarse, un día tras otro, sin cenar.» [21] Although he is not blind to the material improvements, he is by no means happy with the circumstances of the present. The specter of hunger may be less overpowering, but so long as it exists in any form, Cela cannot relax his sword arm.

Although this book gives birth to several unique figures who are worthy of being included in the unforgettable gallery of grotesqueness, [22] for the most part, the new characters constitute a synthesis of the old. Possibly, Cela's well of creative travels has run dry? Certainly, we have the impression that his efforts are superimposed on him, either by a sense of duty or by a desire to maintain his reputation as the explorer of Spain. The fact is that he practically overreaches himself in attemptiong to create new characters. In *Primer Viaje Andaluz* the projection of the author as a literary entity is more forceful, but less real than in his other books of travels. In a word, it seems contrived.

When the author alluded to his romantic interlude with a widow in *Judios, Moros y Cristianos*, the reader was experiencing a novelistic situation. Beyond having the identity of the author, Cela was a multidimensional protagonist in a fictionalized account. He was the dashing hero who also «olía a muerto». It mattered not whether in fact such an incident had occurred. Its reality rested on literature! However, in *Primer Viaje Andaluz*, his relationship with «la señorita Gracita Garrobo», for all its details, attains a degree of artistic verisimilitude only as it recalls established literary experiences. Thus, as we read the following, we think of Martín Marco and the prostitute who «se durmieron en un abrazo, como dos recién casados».

> La señorita Gracita Garrobo sonrió..., y se quedó dormida como un tronco... El desayuno tuvo su miajita de cachondeo y también sus leves, casi imperceptibles, gotitas de emoción. [23]

---

[21] *Ibid.*, p. 171.

[22] I do not mean to imply any sense of derogation. On the contrary, I consider the term as describing the fulfilment of the author's intention.

[23] *Ibid.*, pp. 266-267.

Similarly, the image of the author as a character comes alive as a woman evokes the «olía a muerto» qualities (now we might say, in the form of «hablaba a muerto») of Cela. «—¡Ay, Virgencita del Rosario, que me parece estar oyendo a mi Manuel, que en paz descanse!» [24]

Fundamentally, for Cela there is little to discover in Andalusia. The incantation to Sevilla, for example, has become commonplace. «Sevilla ha sido ya cantada en todos los tonos y con todos los adjetivos nobles.» [25] For the most part, we have the well-known banal types, already described by others. It is only when we come face to face with unique characters who could be *gallegos* or *castellanos* as well as *andaluces* that our fervor is rekindled. Thus, the author's experiences with doña Mencía Corrales, with «Heliodoro, algo poeta», with «don Jacinto Camarón, medio poeta», and with don Roque, also known as «el Espantible», to name a few, bring a spark of Cela's creativity.

Doña Mencía Corrales, «una señorita más que sesentona» [26] (Cela is fascinated by celibacy) charms with her frankness. She has not lost her desire to be a woman; nor does she mask her destiny with the pretense of virtue. Romantic words move her; amorous exclamations excite her. «A doña Mencía Corrales—se le notaba en la mano—le subió la temperatura.» [27] Doña Mencía Corrales perfoms the unexpected role of a young *señorita* with the dignity of an old one. Although Cela preserves his materialistic position («Doña Mencía Corrales, cuando se repuso, sacó unas pastas y unas copitas de vino dulce. El vagabundo—sin precipitarse, que siempre es incorrecto—se comió cuarenta pastas, sobre poco más o menos») [28] when they part, Cela is left not only with a superb gift of food but also with noble thoughts: «¡Dios la bendiga!, se mereciera eso y mucho más.» [29]

Heliodoro is «algo poeta» and also somewhat of a practical man. «—Mi señora que se llama María, como mi pueblo, pero sin santa, y fue de la vida, como somos todos, ejerce de partera sin licencia...» [30] His rewarding marriage affords him the luxury of writing verses. Since he works for the railroad, his muse has two faces: «No, señor,

---

[24] *Ibid.*, p. 202.
[25] *Ibid.*, p. 249.
[26] *Ibid.*, p. 230.
[27] *Ibid.*, p. 232.
[28] *Ibid.*, p. 231.
[29] *Ibid.*, p. 233.
[30] *Ibid.*, p. 346.

yo no hago más que versos de dos clases: espirituales y ferroviarios.» [31] Heliodoro maintains a sense of logical proportion between materialism and art. The author soon learns to integrate into Heliodoro's world.

>—¿Quiere usted que le diga uno ferroviario? si me dice que sí, le invito a comer y le presento a mi señora.
>—¡Hombre, claro! ¡Iba a decírselo yo! [32]

Don Jacinto Camarón is «medio poeta» not because of his attitude, but rather because of the quality of his verses. Actually, his position before life is most poetic. He is intransigent. He refuses to compromise with his destiny. Hungry though he is, he will not debase himself by borrowing from neighbors. The author, whose idealism is less abstract, offends with his practicality.

>—Don Jacinto, le traigo tres peces de regalo...
>—Gracias, mi buen amigo y favorecedor; lo malo es que no tengo ni una gota de aceite para freírlos...
>—¿Y por qué no le pide un poco prestado a algún vecino?
>Don Jacinto Camarón abrió los ojos como un buho; a los poetas, cuando se les suelta la dignidad, se les abren unos ojos grandes y redondos, pasmados y mansos y dolorosos.
>—¿Yo?
>—Sí, usted.
>Al vagabundo, con un severo gesto y muy pocas palabras, lo echaron a la calle.
>—Salga usted de esta casa sin perder ni un momento, es lo único que tengo que decirle.
>—Bueno, pero me llevo los peces. [33]

The characterization of Roque Redondo Méndez encompasses several dimensions of identity. Obssessed with the idea of becoming *don* Roque, «por eso de que llegó durante la guerra a brigada de intendencia»,[34] the poor man who wants to live in the «glory» of a past war, only succeeds in obtaining an ignominous alias. The more intense his desire to be a *don*, the more the townspeople of Cartaya insist

---

[31] *Ibid.*, p. 347.
[32] *Ibid.*, p. 347.
[33] *Ibid.*, pp. 127-128.
[34] *Ibid.*, p. 375.

on calling him «Espantible». His threats, like his dream, remain unfulfilled.

>—¡Al primero que me llame *Espantible* lo mato!—dijo don Roque un día que se ajumó.
>Desde entonces, claro es, le llama *Espantible* todo el mundo. Que el vagabundo sepa, don Roque todava no mató a nadie.[35]

The author, in the role of a Sansón Carrasco, or a malicious innkeeper, capitalizes on Roque's dream of reverence by addressing him repetitively as «don Roque». The knighting of Roque is no less cynical than that of Don Quijote. In an act of repercussion the author continues to refer to the character as «Espantible».

>—¡Qué gordo está usted, don Roque, y qué buen pelo cría!...
>*Espantible* puso un gesto de tonto de escalafón... Qué, ¿me acepta usted otra copita?
>—¡Hombre, don Roque, no le voy a desairar a usted![36]

Thus, the transference of personalities is rendered void. As for the momentary literary identity of the author himself, there is no greater nobility than satisfying one's hunger, «la única causa noble para no comer es la de no tener qué comer...»[37]

Before undertaking his trip to the south of Spain, as Cela dreamed of his past exploits, a serious act of «knighting» did take place *in absentia*. «...si Dupont no se hubiera marchado a su país, tenía—el vagabundo—pensado armarle caballero, como a Don Quijote lo armaron...»[38] The world needs miraculous feats, even if they are trivial. «El vagabundo piensa que, con Dupont a la vera, los niños de Ostiz hubieran visto hacer verdaderas maravillas a su cometa.»[39] The role of the author as a literary character, however, oscillates between the extreme poles of practicality and idealism. Dupont has left him. Cela must play two parts, his and that of the benign Frenchman. Although both identities are often merged into one, mostly Cela excells

---

[35] *Ibid.*, p. 375.
[36] *Ibid.*, p. 375.
[37] *Ibid.*, p. 377.
[38] *Ibid.*, p. 27.
[39] *Ibid.*, p. 33.

as a character who thrives on the fantasies of others. Of course, in the case of doña Mancía Corrales the process was reversed. Myth was created out of the fabric of cruel reality. On the other hand, tourists do not inspire such treatment. Neither does the Vatican.

> En la plaza del Pan, una turista sueca que estaba como un tren dio un duro al vagabundo porque se dejase retratar con ella. El vagabundo, claro es, cogió su duro, pero pensó que estas mujeres nórdicas—que suelen estar que no se las salta un banderillero—tienen la rara costumbre de pagar dinero por determinados servicios que los españoles solemos prestar gratis y tan honrados como agradecidos.
> —Y ahora, del brazo.
> —Eso son dos duros, señorita. En España es muy arriesgado retratarse del brazo con una extranjera. Está prohibido por el concordato, ¿sabe usted? [40]

Again, as in times past, the government of the *caudillo* is the object of piercing ridicule. As the years go by, Cela's attitude toward humanity softens, but his criticism of the Spanish regime becomes more relentless. Only an infinite sense of humor restrains Cela from taking a virulent position. Cela finds comedy even in pathos. Moreover, in the process of finding absurdities, he does not free himself. He is a part of the whole, an active part at that. He neither wishes nor can he escape punishment. Thus, as he recites verses of the Reconquest, when Moors were enemies, he is reminded by a guard that in the last «Crusade» [41] Moors were on the right side. They fought side by side with the Generalissimo, as did Cela. «El guardia, mirando para otro lado, intentó decir algo trascendente. —Y con los moros, menos coñas, que fueron nuestros hermanos de armas en la Cruzada. ¿Me entiende? —Sí, señor, sí.» [42] In another significant incident Cela must prove by virtue of his papers that he is a loyal Spanish subject, in effect, a good security risk. In *La Colmena,* not having these precious papers proved to be Martín Marco's undoing.

---

[40] *Ibid.,* pp. 270-271.
[41] Previously, the author had ironically expressed his vision of *Crusades.* «...los caballeros cruzados, sin mala voluntad y quizá no más que por distraerse y no perder el entreno, empezaron a matar judíos...» *Ibid.,* p. 123.
[42] *Ibid.,* p. 59.

El guardia civil miró para el vagabundo.
—¿Es usted súbdito español?
—Sí, señor, la mar de súbdito, se lo juro... Mire usted, aquí tengo la cédula... Ahí lo dice...
—Entonces, ¿por qué anda usted contando que es búlgaro de detrás del telón de acero?
El vagabundo sintió de repente un violento, un despiadado picor en el ojete.
—¡Responda usted y no se rasque!
—Es que me pica mucho, señor guardia... Me pica un horror..., a veces me pasa...[43]

«Me pica mucho» and especially the «me pica un horror...» reveal more than a mere *itch*. The stylistic meaning implies that he is hurt, that he has been wounded. Subsequently, as he is asked whether he is Russian, or French of Portuguese, he retorts: «—No... Yo, no decírselo a nadie, soy un espía polaco que se bebe la sangre de los niños...»[44] If he is to be an alien in *Andalucía*, he might as well be an exotic one.

As a novelist, Cela is aware of the many meanings of a word or an utterance. His literary characters, himself included, express not only what they are but also what they think they are. In fact, their reality rests on both states, being and wanting to be. And Cela captures their complex human essence, often without developing their personalities. The fleeting moment suffices for the fractional operation. Many times we do not even know their names, and have but a vague impression of their persons. However, we do penetrate their disproportionate lives. Thus, as a woman accepts two fish in exchange for cooking a third for the author, she proudly but erroneously insists that she is guided by charity: «—Por caridad se lo hago, sólo por caridad».[45] However, when she again employs the phrase «por caridad», her act of kindness has an air of pure love. She gives him a place to sleep. And this was not part of the bargain.

As an historian, the author recognizes that purity of facts is not what the readers seek. They want history to reflect the image they have of their nation, their religion, «Esta fábula de los santos beligerantes, que tan poco tiene que ver con el cristianismo, goza de mucho

---

[43] *Ibid.*, pp. 342-343.
[44] *Ibid.*, p. 343.
[45] *Ibid.*, p. 129.

predicamento entre las gentes cristianas.» [46] Cela fills their needs without sacrificing thuth. Even if it is classified as such, legend is intertwined with the telling of history. Whether the Spanish reader will find the ultimate form of legend, palatable, as it is reduced to the realm of experience, is another matter. Much will depend on the individual proclivities of the reader. One can be reasonably certain, however, that the government «Institutos» will not invite Cela to write school texts of history.

In *Judíos, Moros y Cristianos* Cela had maintained a nearly serious position while trying to establish himself as an historian. In *Primer Viaje Andaluz* his role of historian is more secure. No strain is evident in his efforts. He need not dramatize his scholarly accomplishments. Thus, it is in a mood of nonchalance that he improves on the Royal Academy Dictionary by including a vocabulary of *andalucismos* not found in the learned book. History too is recited with the simple arrogance that characterizes the erudite vagabond. A note of ridicule further identifies the style of the author. Cela has no sense of absolute reverence, least of all for scholars. The fact that the author is now himself a scholar only serves to increase the perspective of absurdity. «El origen y la antigüedad de Osuna se pierden en la noche de los tiempos. Los historiadores, cuando no saben una cosa, que es con bastante frecuencia, dicen esto de la noche de los tiempos.» [47]

Primer Viaje Andaluz may very likely be not only the «último viaje andaluz» but the last of Cela's books of travels. Throughout the account of his peregrination South, one senses the author's weariness. In the role of a vagabond, Cela seems to have exhausted his exploration of Spain. He no longer feels at home in the garments of a hobo. For one thing, he now has a «patria chica», as it were, a base of operations, Palma de Mallorca. The Peninsula has become a remote market place where business is transacted with publishers, and an exclusive country club where he enjoys the privileges of an Academician. The fear of recognition is always present. Many towns which were at one time recondite and isolated now maintain open communication with the large cities of Spain. To be sure, clandestine travel would still be possible for the author, but the procedure might demand a burdensome disguise. His only escape might be to assume the identity

---

[46] *Ibid.*, p. 126.
[47] *Ibid.*, pp. 227-228.

of one of the many bourgeois travellers. The fate that awaits Cela is the fate that befell Martín: no longer could he be «Martín, el de las alpargatas»; he would now have to become «Martín, el de la moto».

The creativity of Cela must find new expressions. From disparate drama that is life, Cela will undoubtedly continue to shape a new literature. He is not committed to form. He adheres to no movements. The burning question is whether he can forge art in the comfort of a picturesque study overlooking the Mediterranean. Only time can tell whether he must again assimilate the mass of humanity that has been the model for his creation or whether he can mold new life from the depot of his experiences.

Genius defies logic. No one can tell, in the last analysis, what form Cela's future writings will take. We can only wonder. However, it would seem reasonable to assume that Spain will continue to be a moving force, an incitement for novelizing life. Cela's total existence is integrated with the circumstances of his nation and its people. Personally and artistically he cannot totally escape the drama of his countrymen—and his own. In his exploration of Spain he has been an actor as well as a producer.

CONCLUSION

Within the framework of Cela's art, it might be considered impertinent to classify his literary productivity as belonging to one genre or another. Cela's «diabolical» intention has been to explode myths, particularly the one relating to «novels». Next to hunger and possibly the Spanish government, the critic occupies the place of honor in Cela's *Inferno*. He might forgive the innocent audience, but not that body of readers who appoint themselves as judges of art by virtue of academic training. We already know how much he disdains «formal scholarship».[1]

Yet, if Cela has chosen to bring «order by disorder»,[2] the critic may be justified in discerning a pattern of literary behavior in artistic expressions which are deliberately disproportionate. Using the broadest possible measures of value one might even categorize the works of Cela quintessentially as novels and books of travels. The rest of his writing, articles, short stories, and collections of inventively grotesque fables, are but fragments, momentary glimpses, of his novels and books of travels.

Cela's preoccupation with Spain constitutes the predominant theme of all his works. His search for Spain is relentless. He seeks to capture the essence of Spanish existence. His quest takes many forms. He cannot exhaust the literary possibilities of recreating life around him. Cela has imposed on himself the fate of Tantalus. But in this sentence the reader shares his agony. The final moment of truth never comes. The experience of living Cela's characters and situa-

---

[1] For the sake of our personal friendship, which I treasure, I can only hope that Cela will count me among the «innocents».

[2] See note 2 chapter XII.

tions is in itself the aesthetic attainment. The problem of Spain is never solved.

In the novels life is objectivized. Spain is but a stage. Contemporary problems are expressed through the creation of literary characters. Circumstances acquire meaning within the personal dramas of Cela's heroes. Their conflicts—often embryonic—overshadow the plight of society. By means of dreams, illusions and fantasies the protagonists transcend their circumscribed possibilities. The acts of rebellion need not be more fully developed than their fragmentary existence. In the horror of hunger, under the surveillance of guns, a groan becomes a roar. In the Spain of the forties the mere pursuit of human dignity was an act of defiance.

In his travels, Cela, himself, as a literary character, weaves the fabric of human existence. The pattern of life is seen through the eyes of the vagabond. He is the inciting force, the prime mover. He is the character in search of a stage. His compulsion to penetrate the inner recesses of Hispanic life motivates his peregrinations. He must experience all possible forms of reality; he must «drink of Spain». The pilgrimage offers no reward other than the palpation of life. In the world of Cela, the act of living is in itself a joyous fulfillment.

Blended with the specter of horror that pervades the works of Cela is a note of poetic imagery that evokes musical exaltation. Songs are shaped from the most trivial aspects of human existence. Cela, the master of horror, is also the master of delicate sensations. He perceives pathos with the same intensity that he dramatizes cruelty. Even in an atmosphere of human depravity, amidst virtual destruction, there are inextinguishable glimmers of man's love. The art of Cela seems to erupt in unexpected disproportion in form as in content. His composition is deliberately grotesque.

As an artist, Cela finds no symmetry in life and he strives to express that image of his experience. The «order» that he championed as a soldier of Franco never attained reality. It disintegrated into chaos at the end of the Civil War. Its fruition was abortive. It evaporated before it could take shape. For Cela, Spain became a symbol of unfulfilment. His literary career, then, begins on the threshold of a frustrated «Crusade». Disillusionment is his Pierian spring. The possession of genius is inexplicable, but its form of expression is inexorably intertwined with the circumstances into which it is born. Cela creates literature out of the rough variegated fabric of Spanish life.

On the whole there is a marked distinction between the acrimonious Cela of the nineteen forties and the ironical Cela of the nineteen fifties. The inherently rebellious spirit of Cela varies in intensity. Maturity has a noticeable influence on his disposition—and his vision of humanity. He does not relent in his criticism, but his mood becomes more temperate. Only hunger remains as his implacable enemy. He can ridicule most everything, even the absurd excesses of his government, but he cannot retain a sense of humor about starvation. In his writings, the ghost of Cela the man cries out for vengeance. There is no mercy for hunger.

In a climate of bourgeois comfort in Palma de Mallorca, removed from the crude texture of Spanish life, Cela assumes a new identity. Amidst the printing presses of his learned journal, *Papeles de Son Armadans,* he forcefully blossoms as a scholar, a philosophical historian of his civilization. There have been no novels since 1954, and his most recent books of travel, *Judíos, Moros y Cristianos* and *Primer Viaje Andaluz* are produced in an aura of creative professional erudition. Cela abandoned the Peninsula not only because of the oppressive atmosphere of censorship, but also as an act of vengeance upon a public that did not wish to understand his work. The art of Cela mirrors the inner truth of the Spanish people, as it captures the essence of post-Civil War life. His novels and books of travels probe too deeply, too painfully. Unquestionably, in his new venture, as an academician, he will arouse less hostility. His own life will be more peaceful, even if readers of literature will be the poorer for it.

The course of Cela's career as an artist has been unpredictably diverse. In a sense, his past cannot be taken as an omen for the future. His genius is explosive. It bursts forth in unexpected forms. It is not unthinkable that he might also become a dramatist. Because the theatre appeals to a selective audience, playwrights enjoy more freedom from censorship than poets and prose writers. On the other hand, his acclaim as a scholar may divert his talent. He will not have been the first writer whose creativity was submerged in a mass of archaelogical pursuits in the role of teacher or editor.

However much one may long for the resumption of Cela's literary adventures (the parasitic critic clamors for art!) it should be noted that already Cela's writings constitute one of the most significant contributions to Spanish literature since the generation of 1898. Almost single handed, Cela resurrected the novel in Spain. To be sure, the genre was not invented by him. There is a bit of the *esperpento* of Valle-Inclán and some vestiges of Baroja's fragmentary style in the prose of Camilo José Cela. Nonetheless, instead of merely reproducing the traditional conflicts of the past, Cela based his novels on his own personal experience of man's agonizing existence. The publication of his first novel, *La Familia de Pascual Duarte,* marked the beginning of a new literary generation. Cela was not afraid to dramatize the plight of his society, living enmeshed in a web of particular circumstances. The protean nature of the novel lent itself to his literary experiment.[3] Out of a degenerate society that groped for survival, Cela forged a new artistic reality. The intense recreation of Spanish life reaches aesthetic heights in the form of characters and situations that reflect the inner truth of man while perpetuating an era of Spanish existence. With intuitive genius Cela molds his art in the image of his society. The explosive shape of his composition conforms to the abortive nature of his times.

---

[3] I am indebted to Professor R. S. Willis of Princeton University for his acute analysis of the novel. In a letter to me he writes: «Novels his [Cela's] long fictions are, though observably different from the 'Classic' novels of Galdós. But the novel, precisely, is a protean form: Cervantes isn't Balzac, who isn't Doestoevsky, Joyce, Mann, Faulkner, etc. The novel, surely, is the artistic expression of the author's intuition of man's living enmeshed in the web of circumstances: with each generation the intuition will change, and the artistic expression will change accordingly, but we still have novels.»

BIBLIOGRAPHY OF CELA'S WORKS IN BOOK FORM, FIRST EDITIONS

(Don Fernando Huarte, a librarian at the National Library in Madrid, will soon publish a complete bibliography *celáyica*. This book will also list the publications which deal with Cela's works.)

Baraja de invenciones, Castalia, Valencia, 1953. 256 pp.
El bonito crimen del carabinero y otras invenciones, Janés, Barcelona, 1947. 163 pp.
Café de artistas, Tecnos, Madrid, 1953. 64 pp. (also included in *El molino de viento y otras novelas cortas*).
Cajón de sastre, Cid, Madrid, 1957. 334 pp.
Historias de Venezuela. La Catira, Noguer, Barcelona, 1955. 405 pp.
Caminos inciertos. La Colmena, Emecé, Buenos Aires, 1951. 252 pp.
Cuatro figuras del 98, Editorial Aedos, Barcelona, 1961. 463 pp.
La cucaña. Memorias de Camilo José Cela, Destino, Barcelona, 1959.
Del Miño al Bidasoa. Notas de un vagabundaje, Noguer, Barcelona, 1952. 275 pp.
Don Pío Baroja, Ediciones de Andrea, México, 1958. 77 pp.
Ensueños y figuraciones, Barcelona, (no date given). 96 pp. (also contained in a later edition of *Mesa revuelta*, Nueva edición aumentada, Taurus, Madrid, 1957. 321 pp.)
Esas nubes que pasan..., Afrodisio Aguado, Madrid, 1945. 179 pp.
La familia de Pascual Duarte, Aldecoa, Madrid, 1942. 190 pp.
El Gallego y su cuadrilla. Y otros apuntes carpetovetónicos, Madrid, 1949. (with the addition of *En el lomo de la cubierta dice*: 1951. 242 pp.)
Historias de España. Los Ciegos. Los tontos, Los Papeles de Son Armadans, Palma de Mallorca, 1957. 24 pp.
Historias de España. Los Ciegos. Los tontos, Arión, Madrid, 1958. 71 pp.
Judíos, moros y cristianos. Notas de un vagabundaje por Ávila, Segovia y sus tierras, Destino, Barcelona, 1956. 309 pp.
Mesa revuelta, Sagitario, Madrid, 1945. 219 pp.
Mis páginas preferidas, Gredos, Madrid, 1956. 414 pp.
El molino de viento y otras novelas cortas, Noguer, Barcelona, 1956. 275 pp.
Mrs. Caldwell habla con su hijo, Destino, Barcelona, 1953. 231 pp.
Nuevas andanzas y desventuras de Lazarillo de Tormes, Juventud (revista semanal), July 4-October 18, 1944. (16 copies.)
Nuevas andanzas y desventuras de Lazarillo de Tormes, La Nave, Madrid, 1944. 316 pp.
Nuevo retablo de don Cristobita. Invenciones, figuraciones y alucinaciones, Destino, Barcelona, 1957.

Pabellón de reposo, El Español (revista semanal), Madrid, March 13-August 21, 1943. (24 copies.)
Pabellón de reposo, Afrodisio Aguado, Madrid, 1943. 157 pp.
Pisando la dudosa luz del día «poesía», Ediciones del Zodíaco, Barcelona, 1945. 94 pp. (Written in Madrid in 1936.)
Primer viaje andaluz. Notas de un vagabundaje por Jaén, Córdoba, Sevilla, Huelva y sus tierras, Noguer, Barcelona, 1959. 468 pp.
La rueda de los ocios, Mateu, Barcelona, 1957. 345 pp.
San Juan de la Cruz, (Written under the pseudonym of Matilde Verdú), Madrid, 1948. 163 pp.
Santa Balbina 37, gas en cada piso, Melilla Mirto y Laurel, 1952. 40 pp. (also included in *El molino de viento y otras novelas cortas.*)
Timoteo, el incomprendido, Rollán, Madrid, 1952. 78 pp. (also included in *El molino de viento y otras novelas cortas.*)
Las botas de siete leguas. Viaje a la Alcarria, Revista de Occidente, Madrid, 1948. 226 pp.
Los Viejos Amigos, Noguer, Barcelona, 1960. 318 pp.

UNIVERSITY OF NORTH CAROLINA
STUDIES IN THE ROMANCE LANGUAGES AND LITERATURES

Urban Tigner Holmes, Jr., *Editor*

Nicholson B. Adams	George Bernard Daniel
Alfred G. Engstrom	William Leon Wiley
Robert W. Linker	Sterling A. Stoudemire

John Esten Keller, *Managing Editor*

Daniel R. Reedy, *Assistant Editor*

Recent Titles

THE EARLY CUADRO DE COSTUMBRES IN COLOMBIA, by Frank M. Duffey. 1956. (Number 26).

THE BOOK OF THE WILES OF WOMEN, translated by John Esten Keller. 1956. MLA Translation Series Number 2. (Number 27). A translation which "supersedes the unsatisfactory translation made by Coote in 1882 for the Folklore Society..." (*Bulletin of Hispanic Studies*).

THE CATHOLIC NATURALISM OF PARDO BAZÁN, by Donald Fowler Brown. 1957. (Number 28).

A BRIEF DESCRIPTION OF MIDDLE FRENCH SYNTAX, by Rosalyn H. Gardner and Marion Green. 1958. (Number 29).

PIERRE BAYLE AND SPAIN, by Kenneth R. Scholberg. 1958. (Number 30).

THE PEREGRINE MUSE, by Robert J. Clements. 1959. (Number 31).

NATURAL HISTORY OF THE WEST INDIES, by Gonzalo Fernández de Oviedo. Translated by Sterling A. Stoudemire. 1959. (Number 32).

MEDIAEVAL LATIN AND FRENCH BESTIARIES, by Florence McCulloch. 1960. (Number 33). A new and stimulating treatment of the genre of the bestiary with references to the great codices.

THE "WISDOM" OF PIERRE CHARRON, An Original and Orthodox Code of Morality, by Jean D. Charron. 1961. (Number 34).

LA CHAÇUN DE WILLAME, edited by Nancy V. Iseley with AN ETYMOLOGICAL GLOSSARY by Guérard Piffard. 1961. (Number 35).

FORMULAIC DICTION AND THE THEMATIC COMPOSITION IN THE "CHANSON DE ROLAND", by Stephen G. Nichols, Jr. 1961. (Number 36).

THE REAPPEARING CHARACTERS IN BALZAC'S COMÉDIE HUMAINE, by Arthur Graves Canfield and edited by Edward B. Ham. 1962. (Number 37).

PIERRE GRINGORE'S LES FANTASIES DE MERE SOTE, ed. by R. L. Frautschi. 1962. (Number 38).

THE SONGS OF BERNART DE VENTADORN, ed. by Stephen G. Nichols, Jr. 1962. (Number 39).

LAS PACES DE LOS REYES Y JUDÍA DE TOLEDO, ed. by James A. Castañeda. 1962. (Number 40).

LA COUR DE GASTON D'ORLEANS, by Claude Abraham. 1963. Pp. 143. (Number 41).

RUTEBEUF AND LOUIS IX, ed. by Edward Billings Ham. 1962. (Number 42).

The University of North Carolina Press
Chapel Hill, North Carolina
European Sales Representative:
Librairie E. Droz, 8 Rue Verdaine, Geneva, Switzerland

www.ingramcontent.com/pod-product-compliance
Lightning Source LLC
Chambersburg PA
CBHW022022220426
43663CB00007B/1175